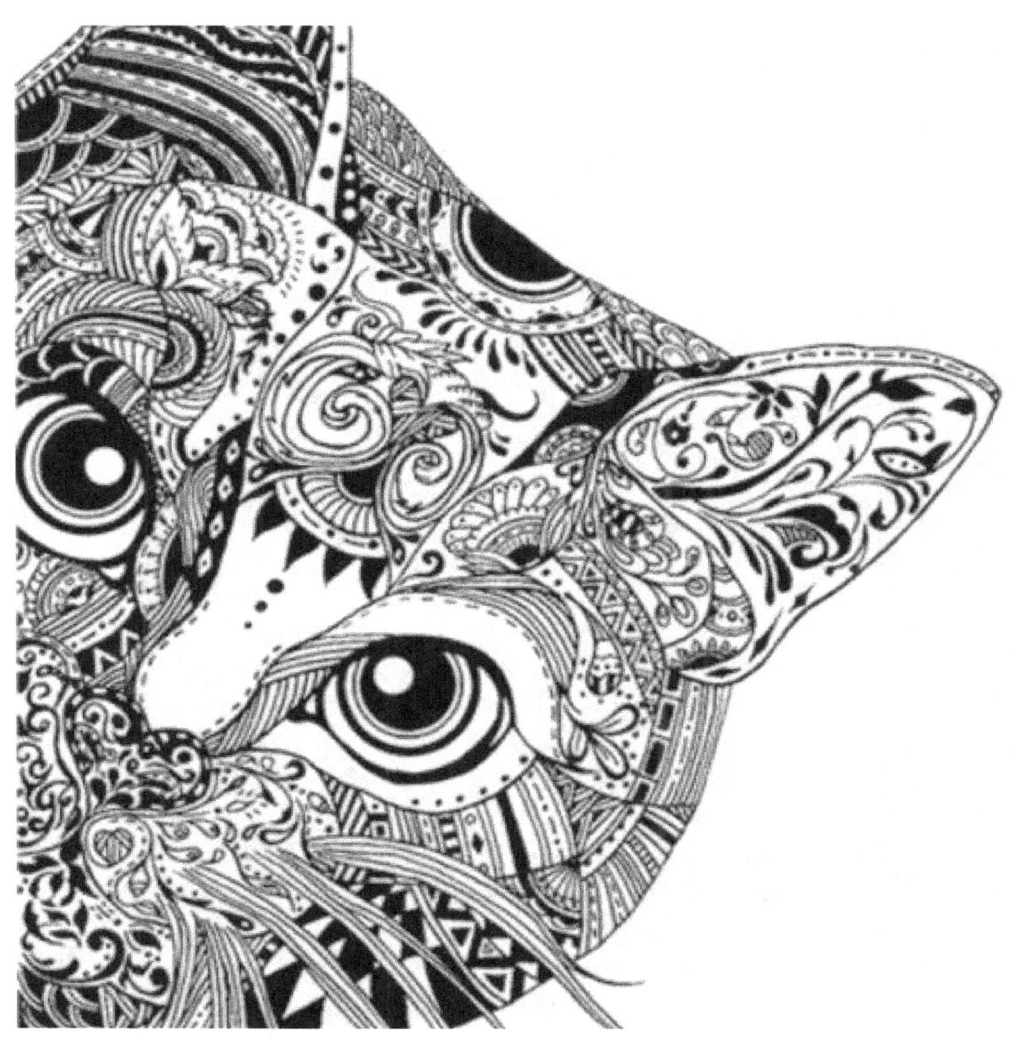

... Energy, meditation, healing

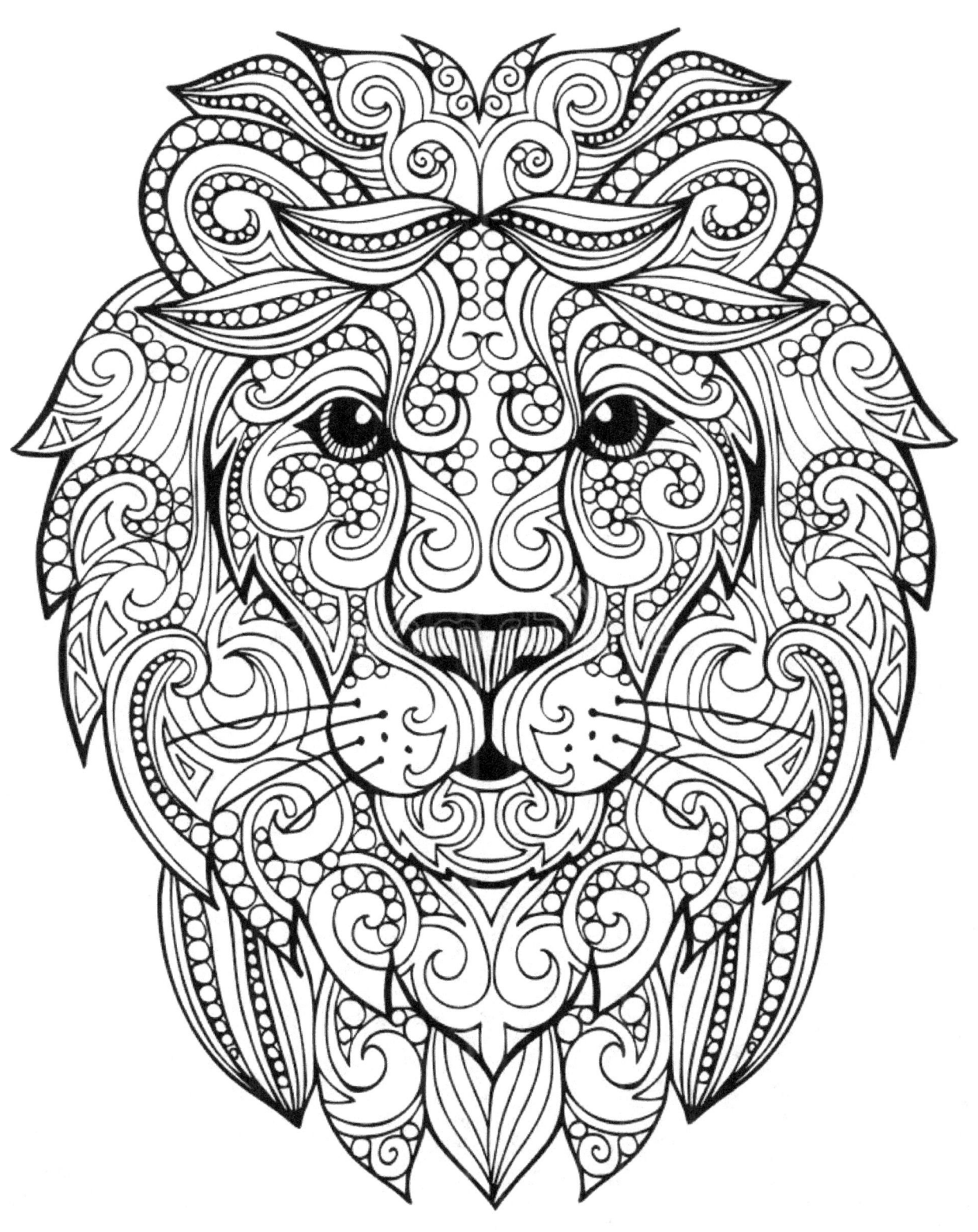

for an inner transformation...

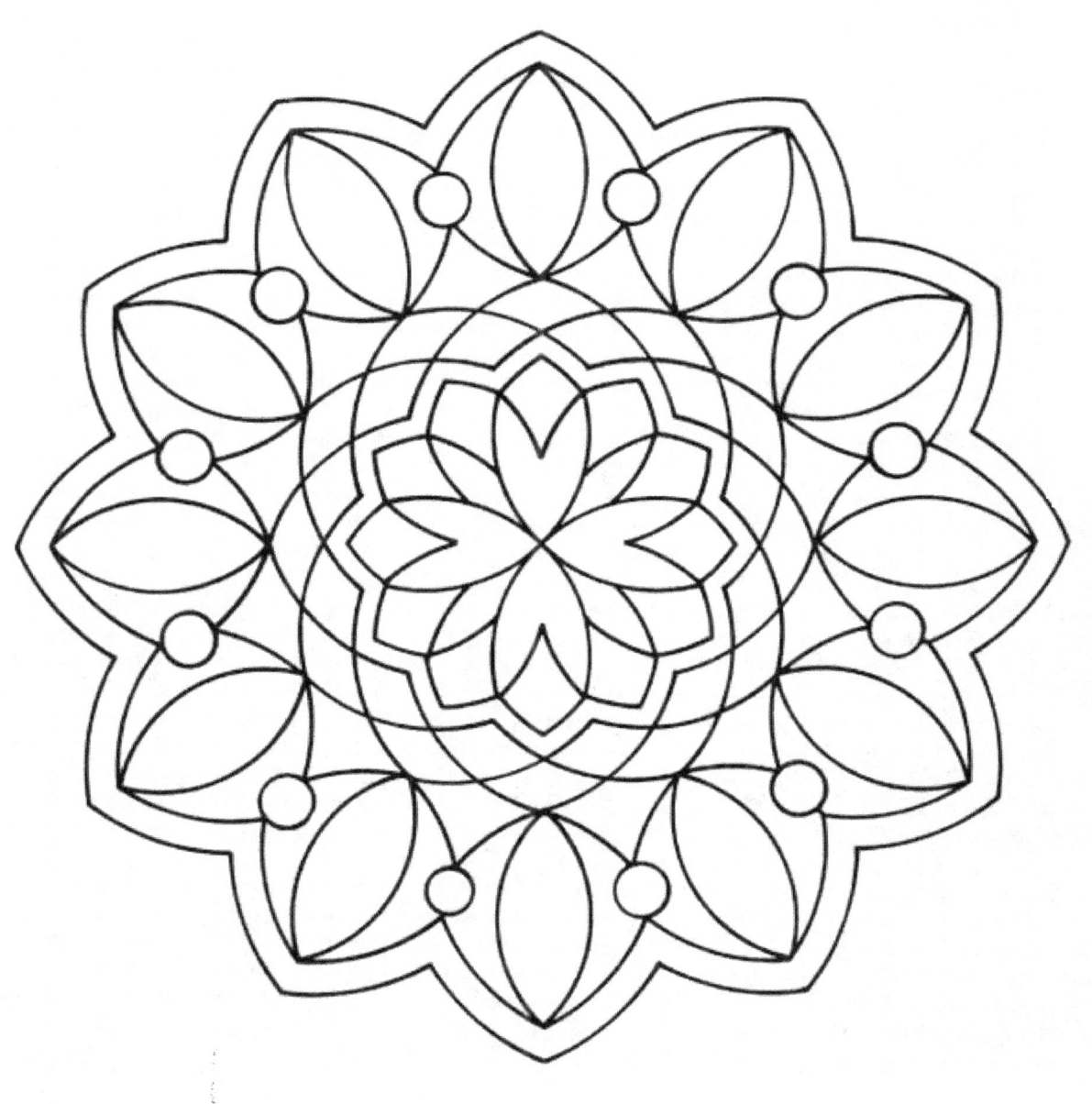

Let's start from here...

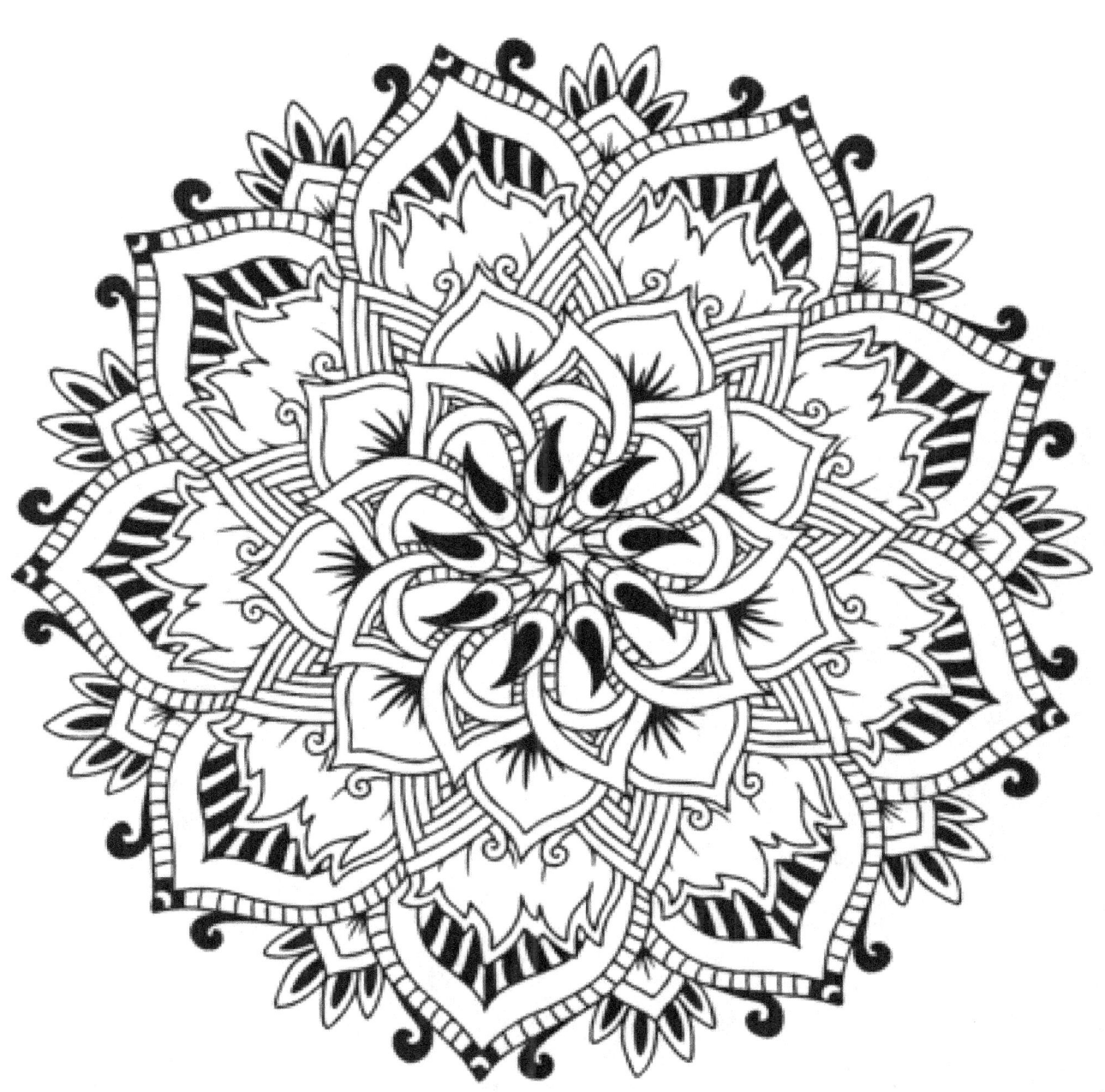

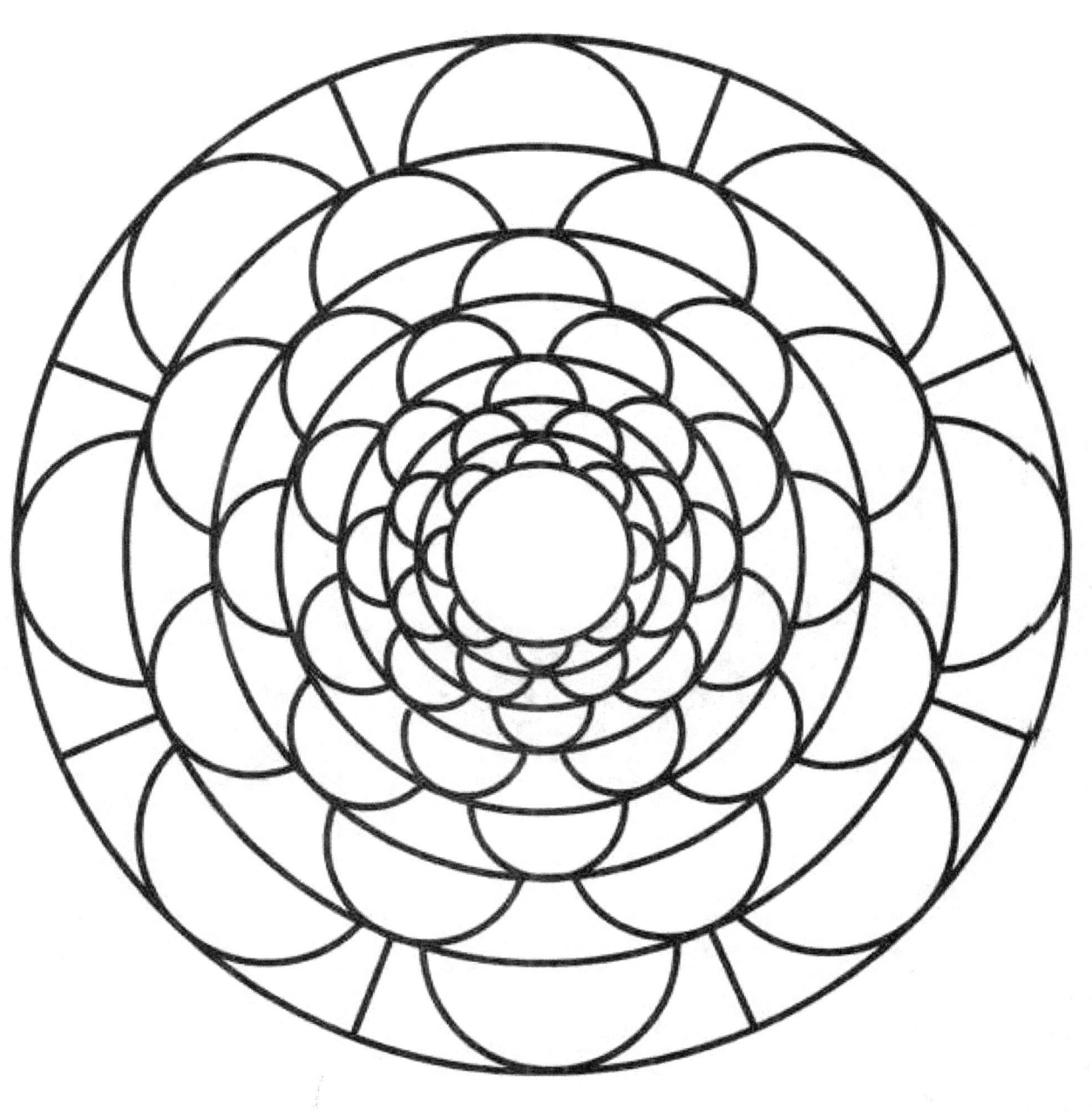

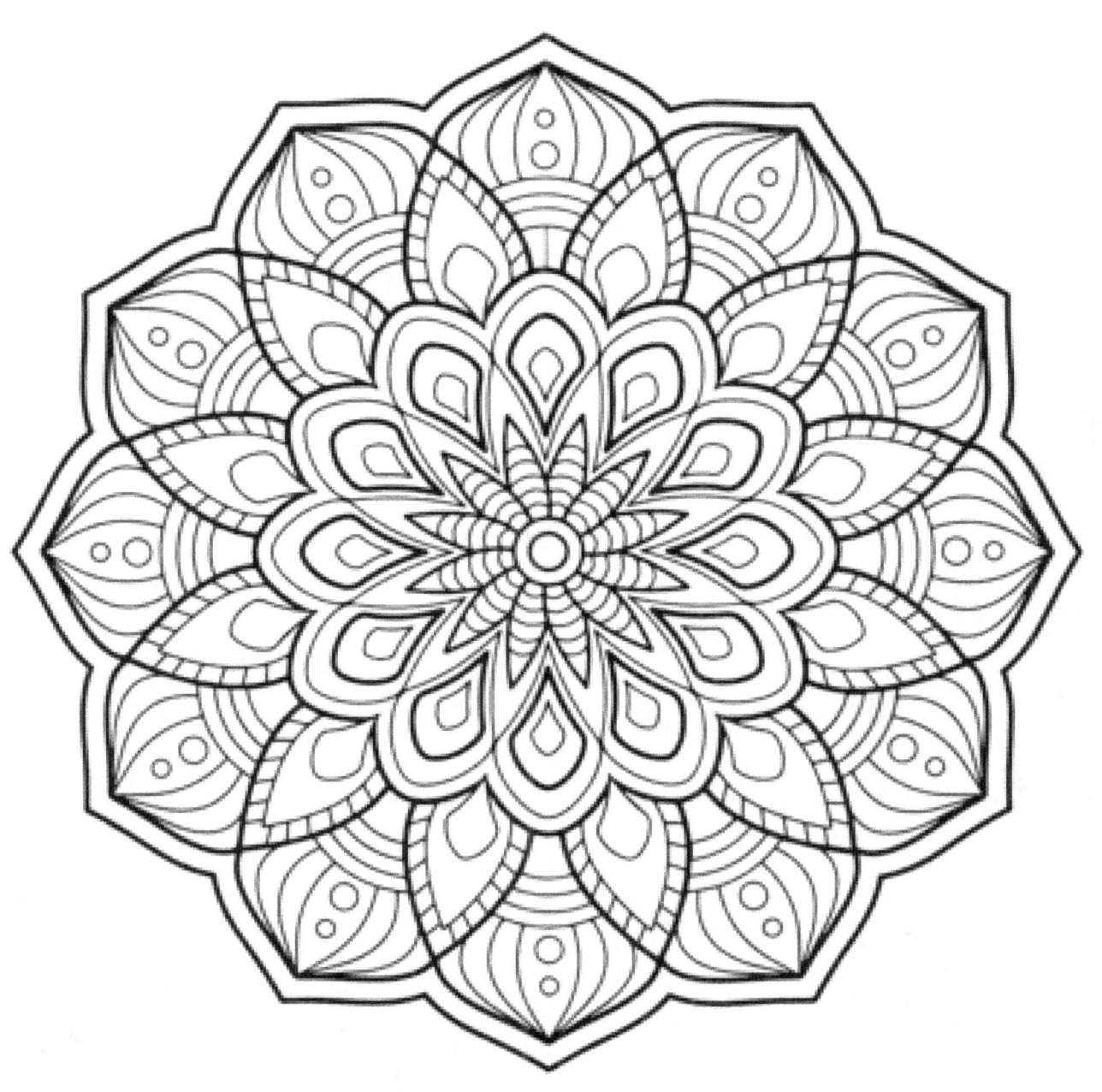

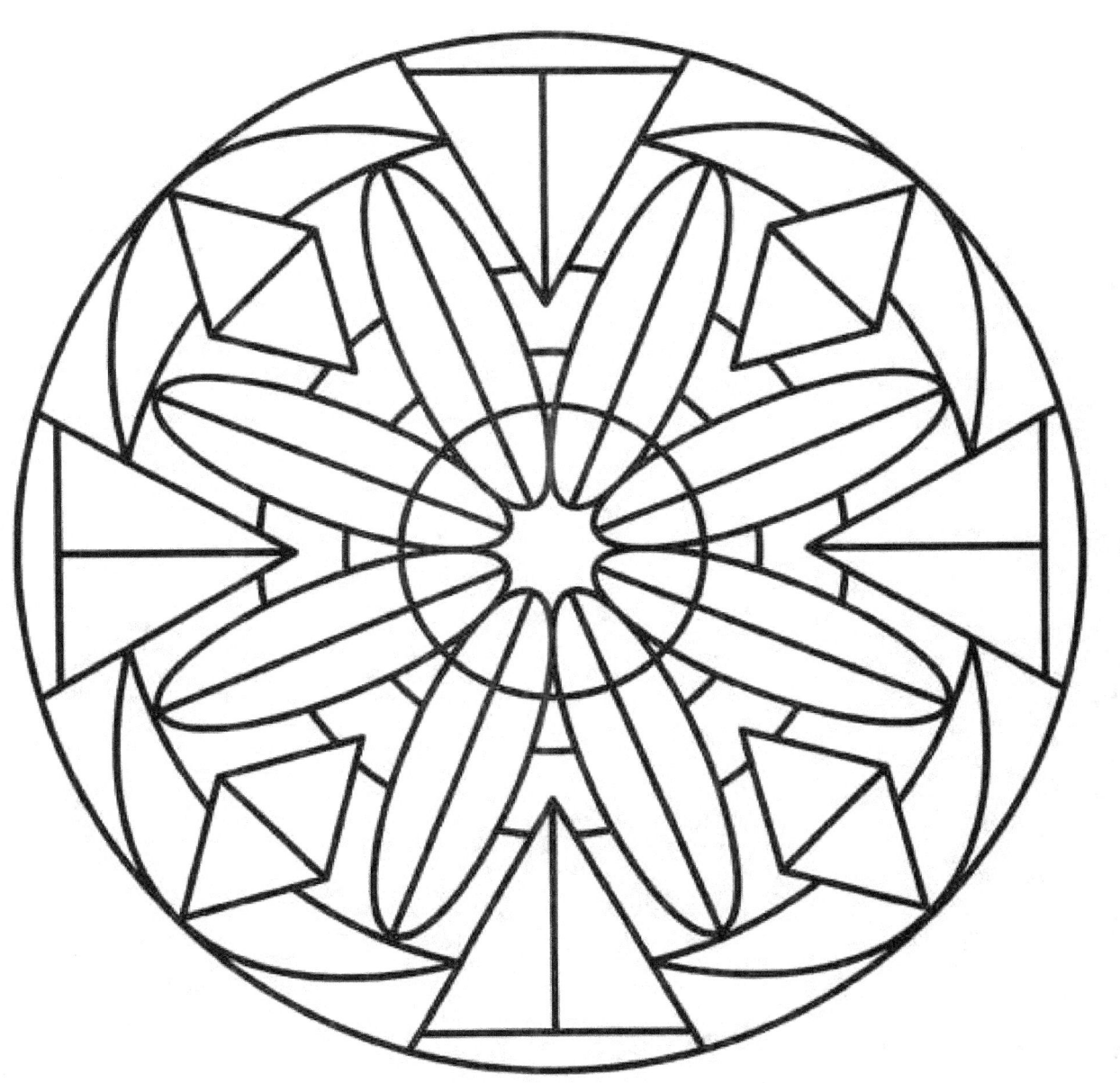

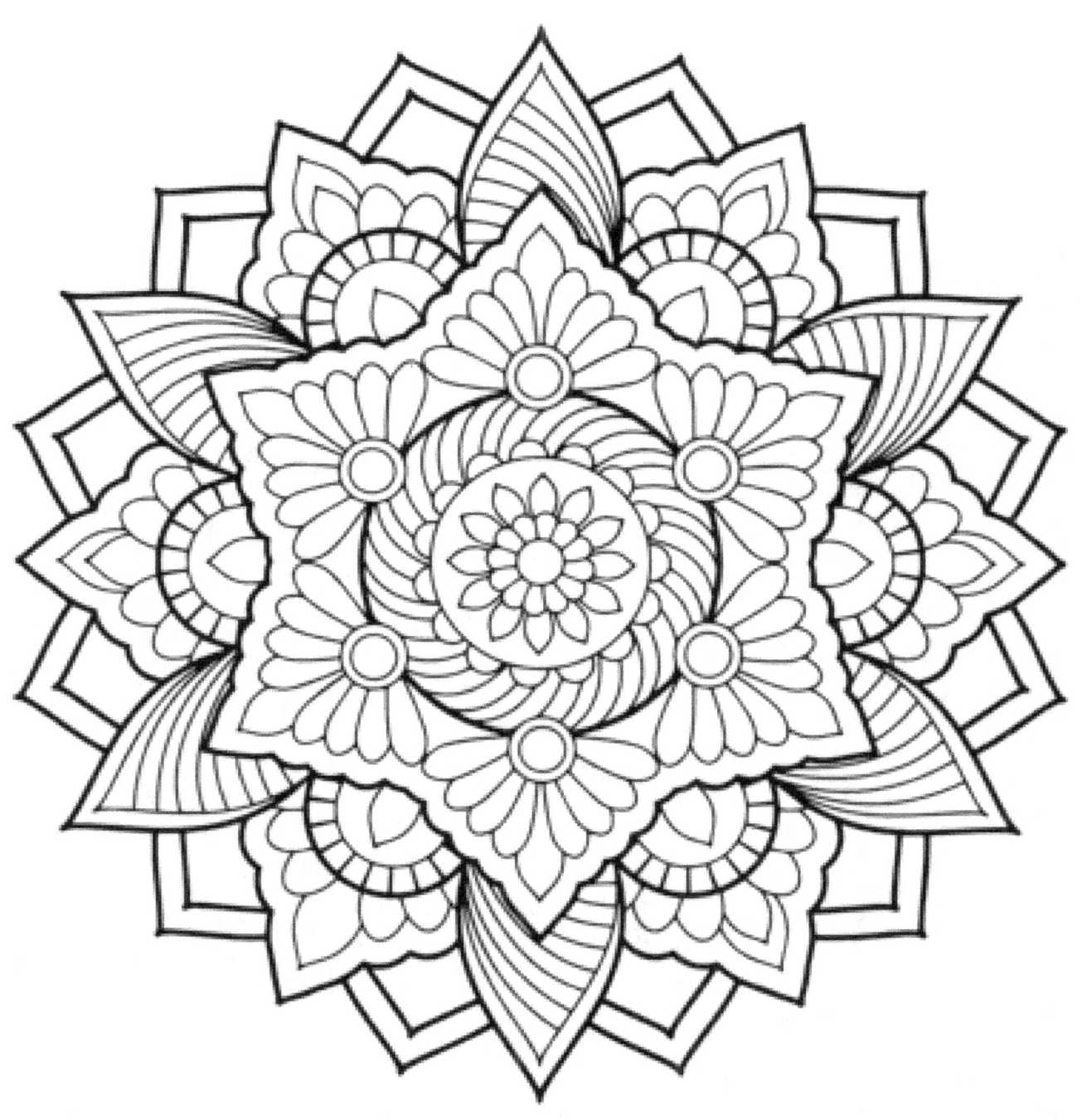

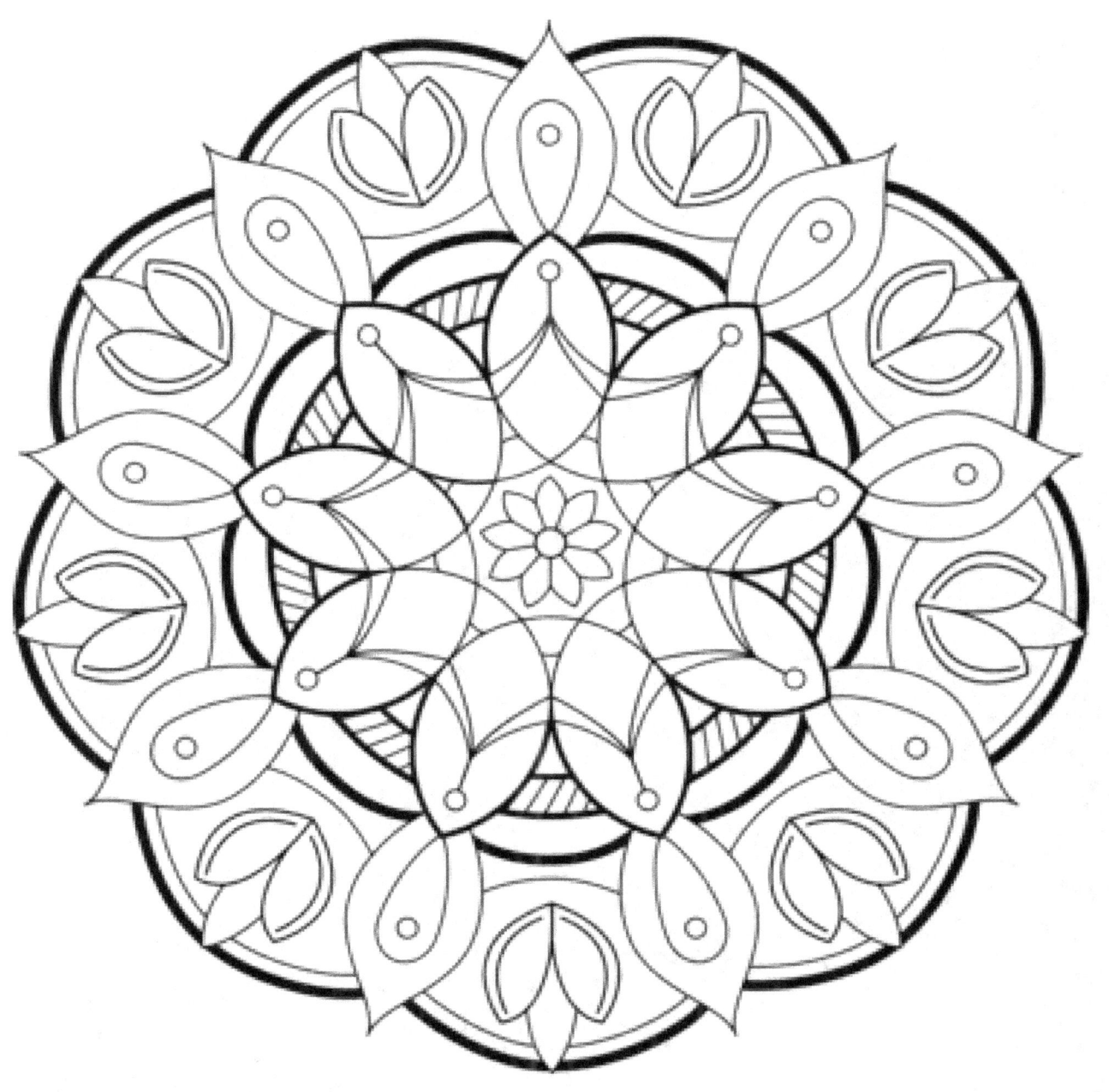

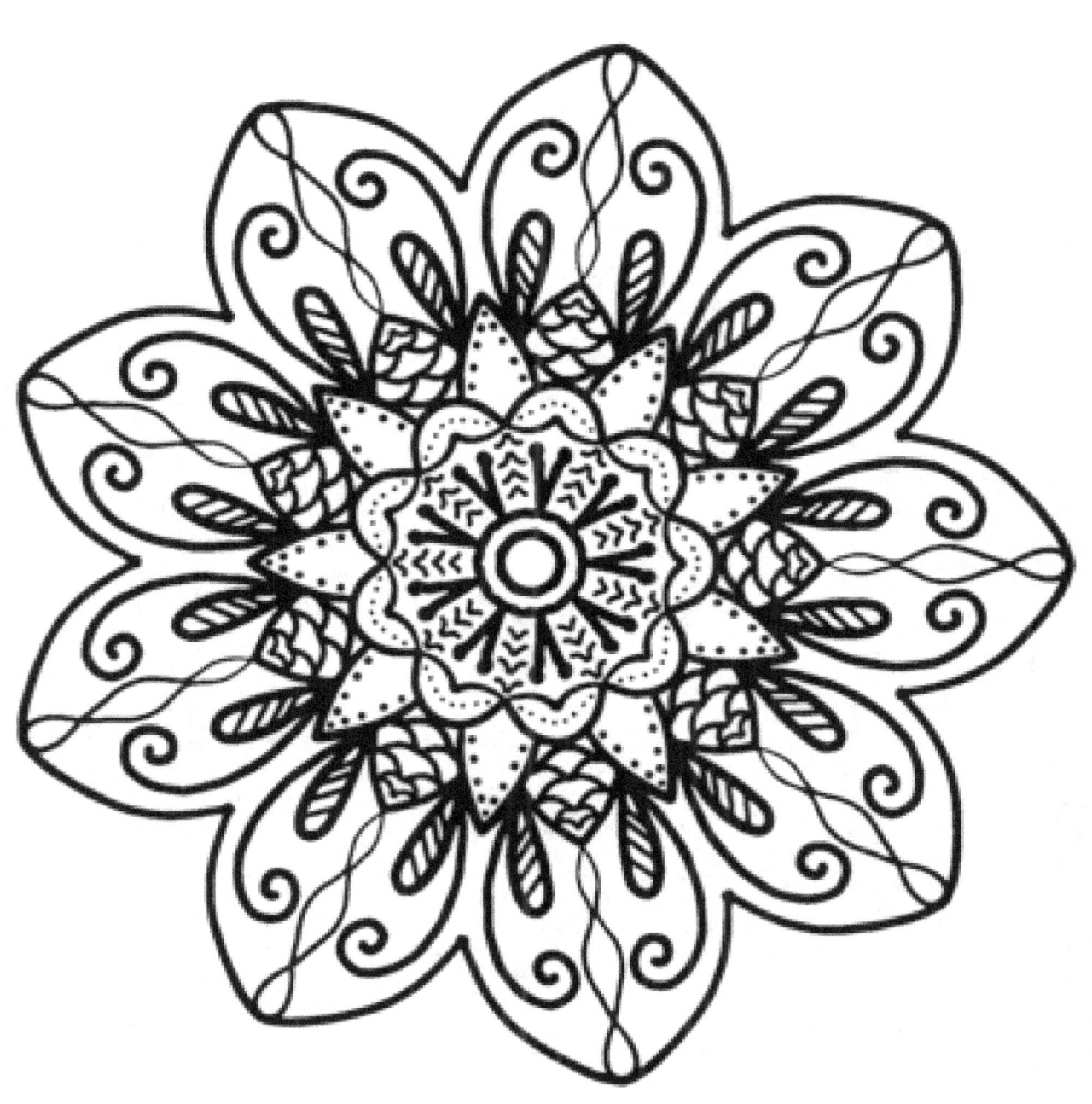

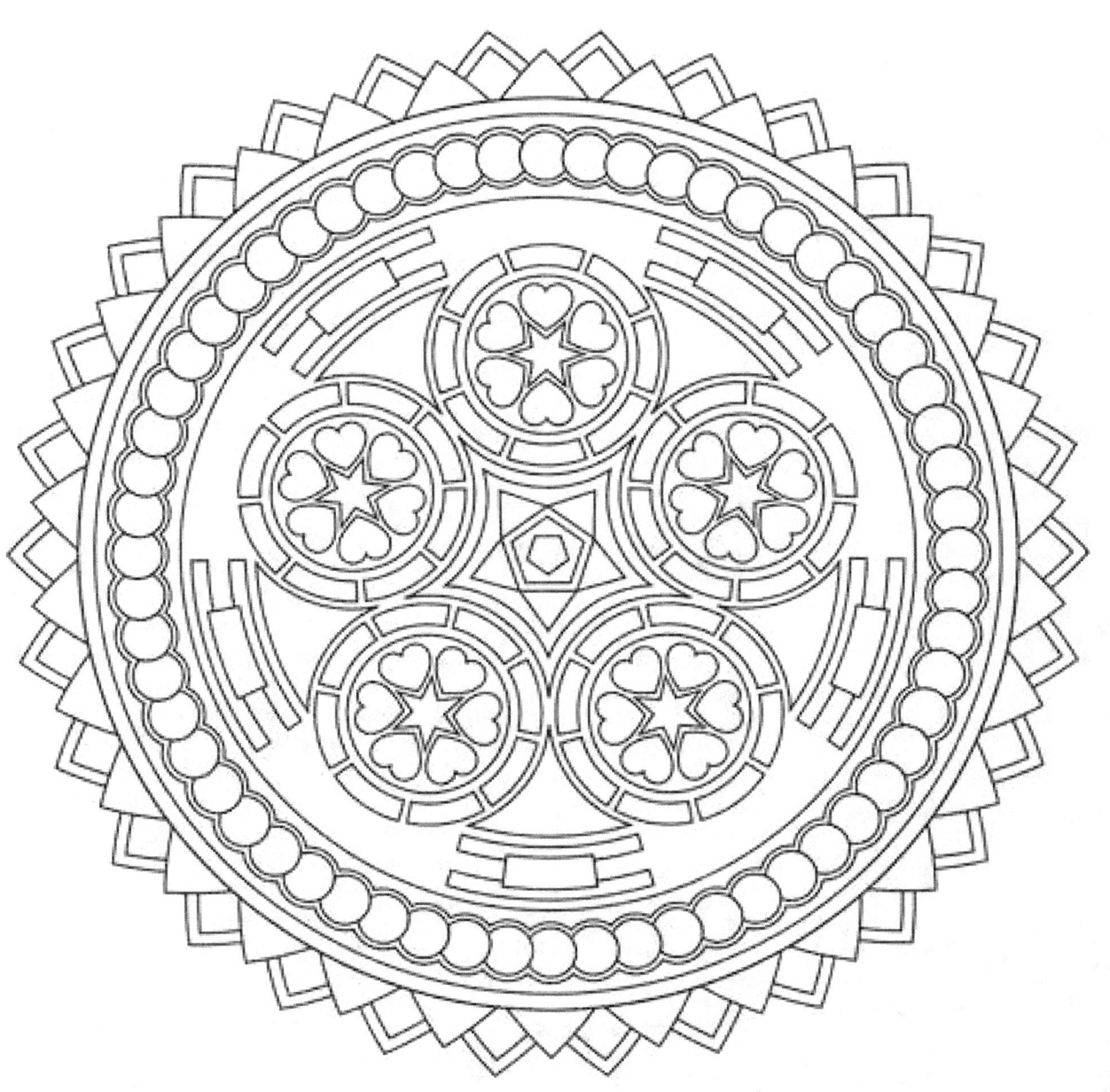

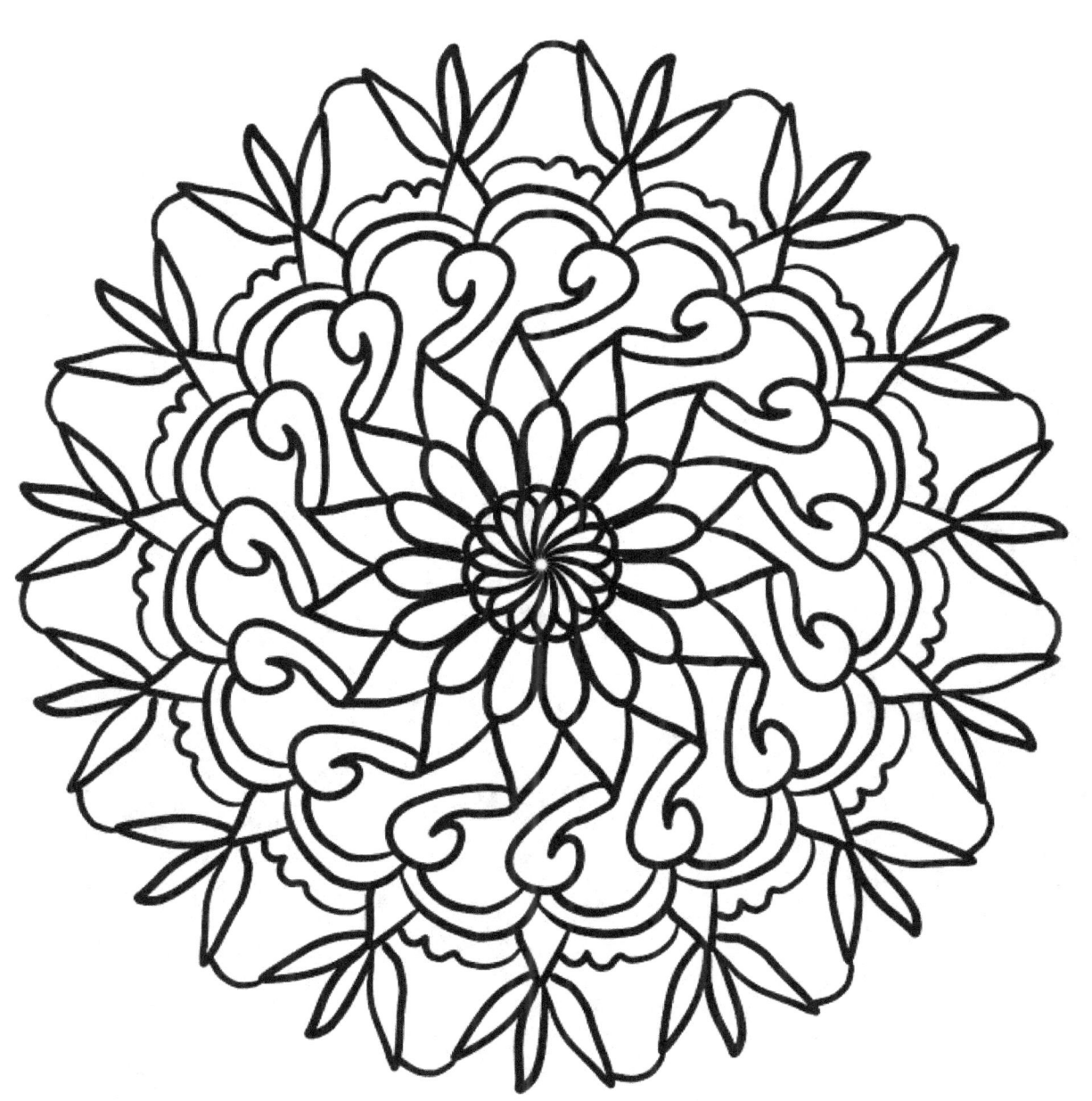

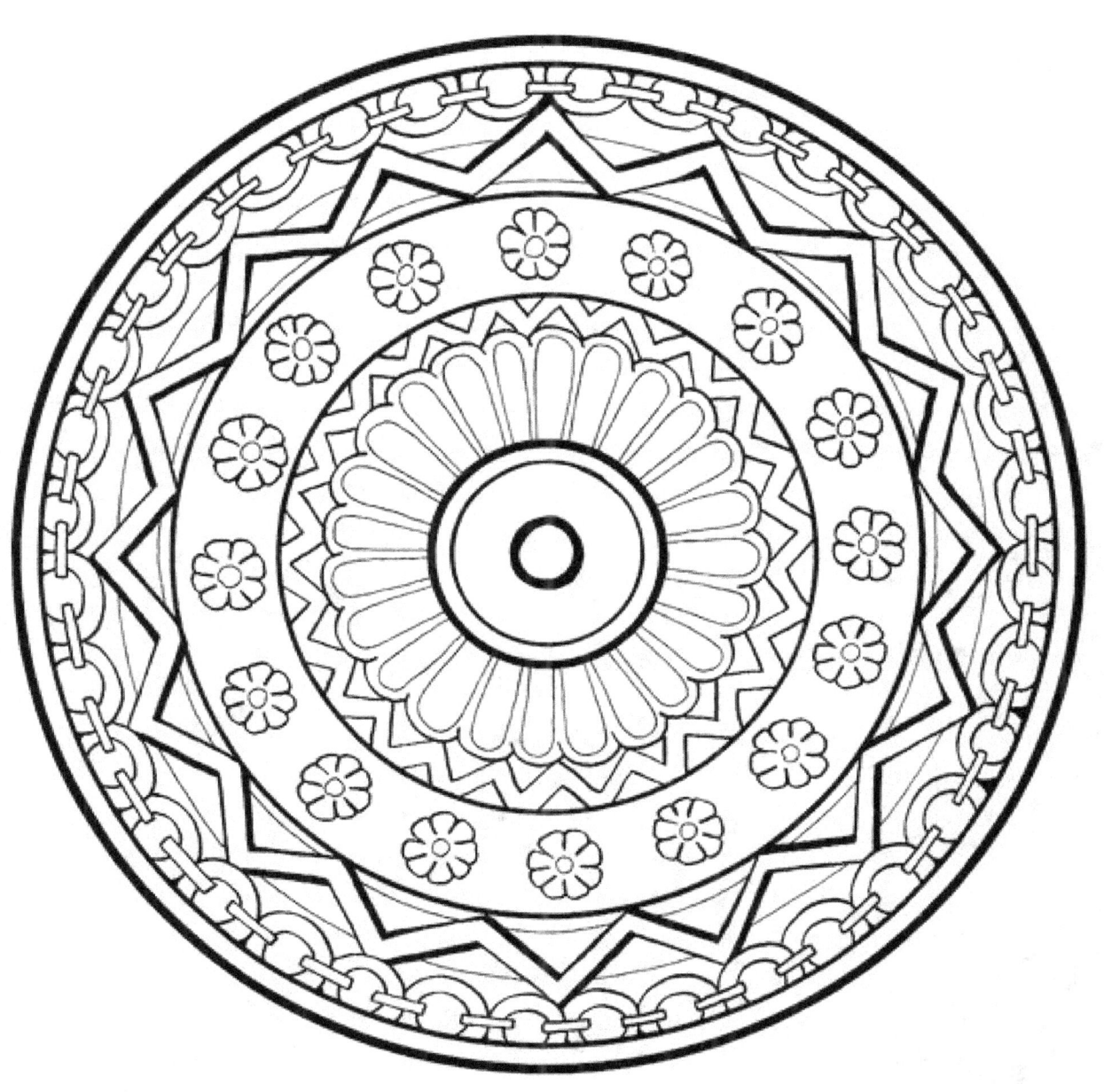

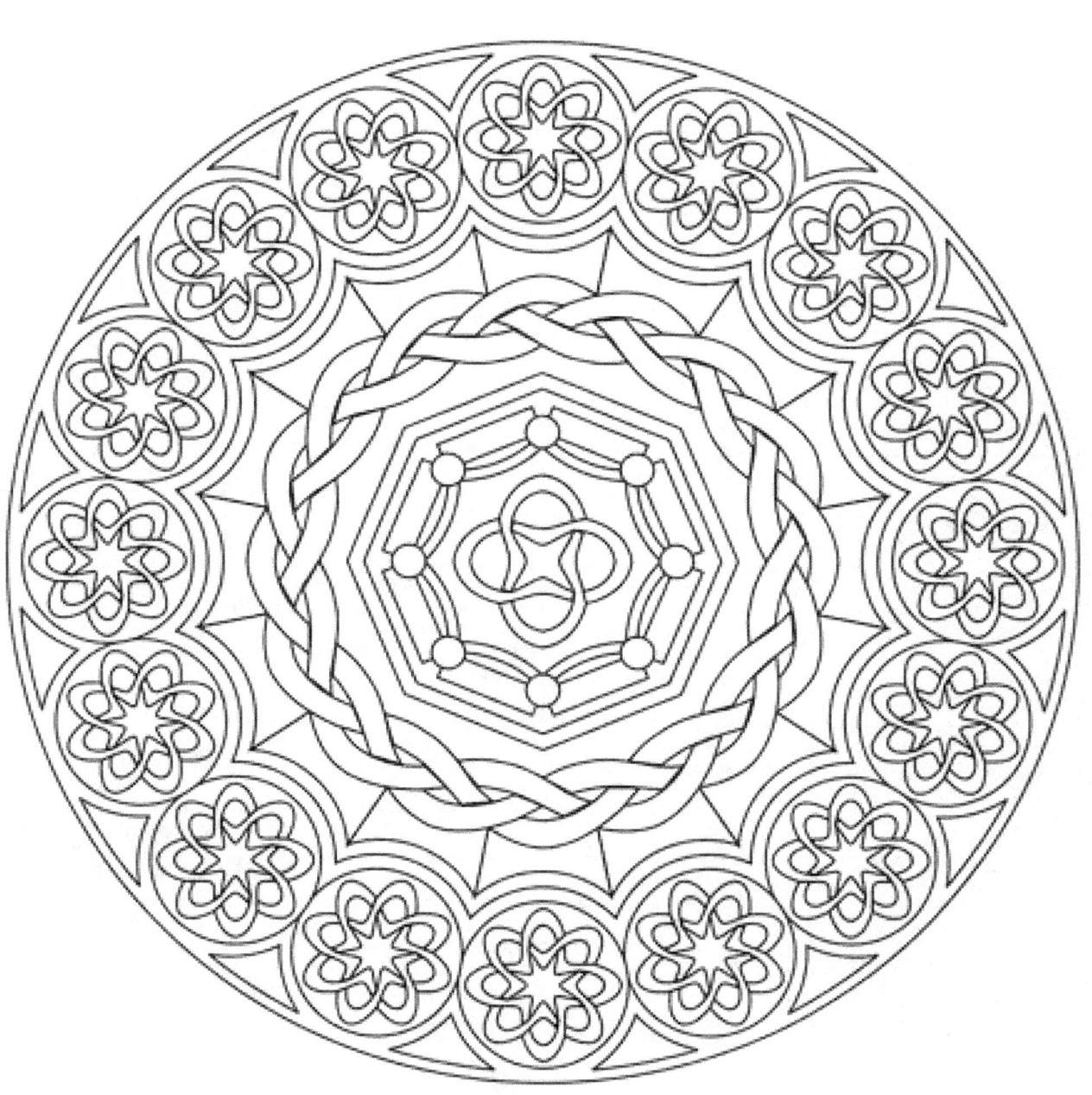

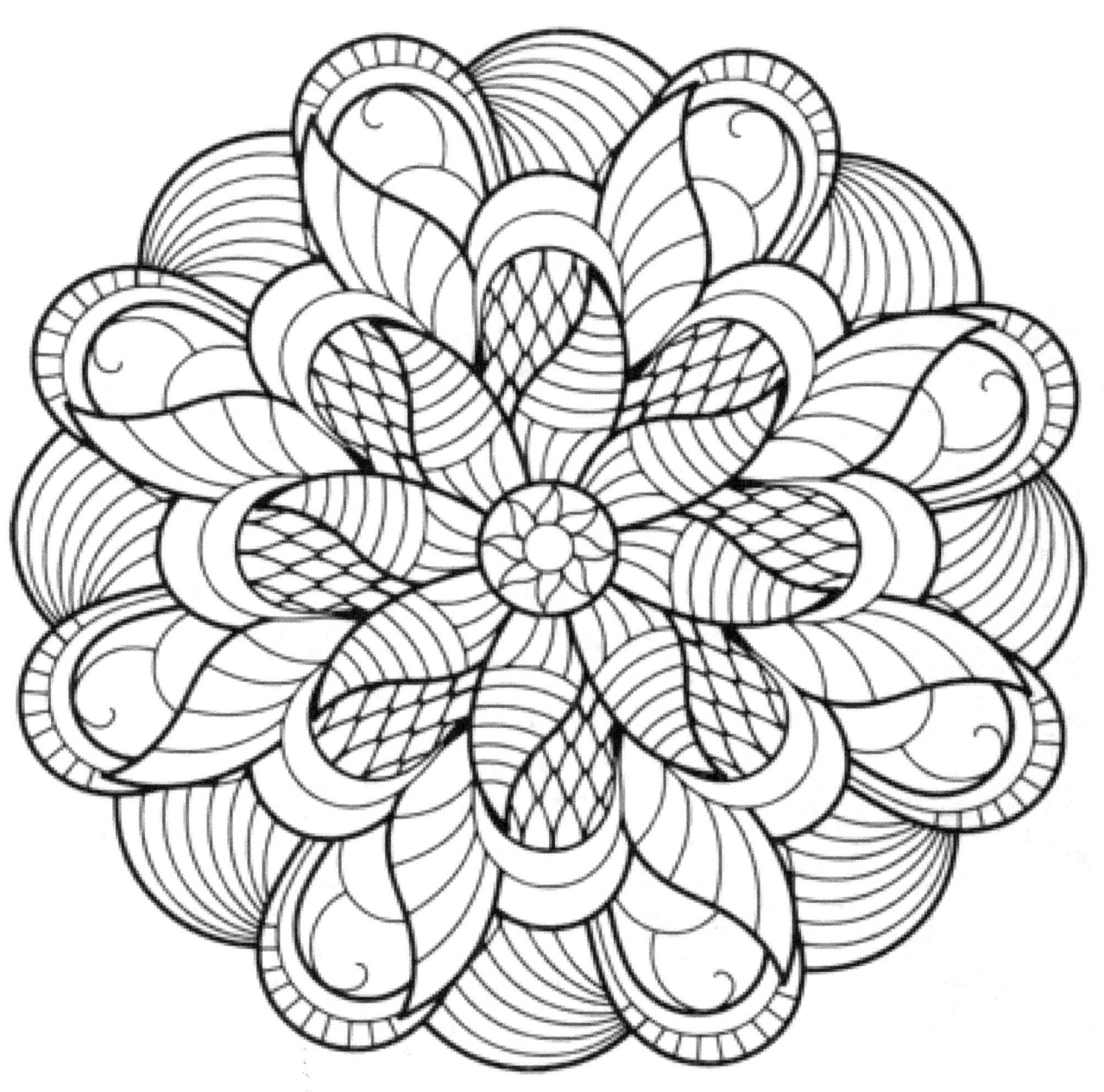

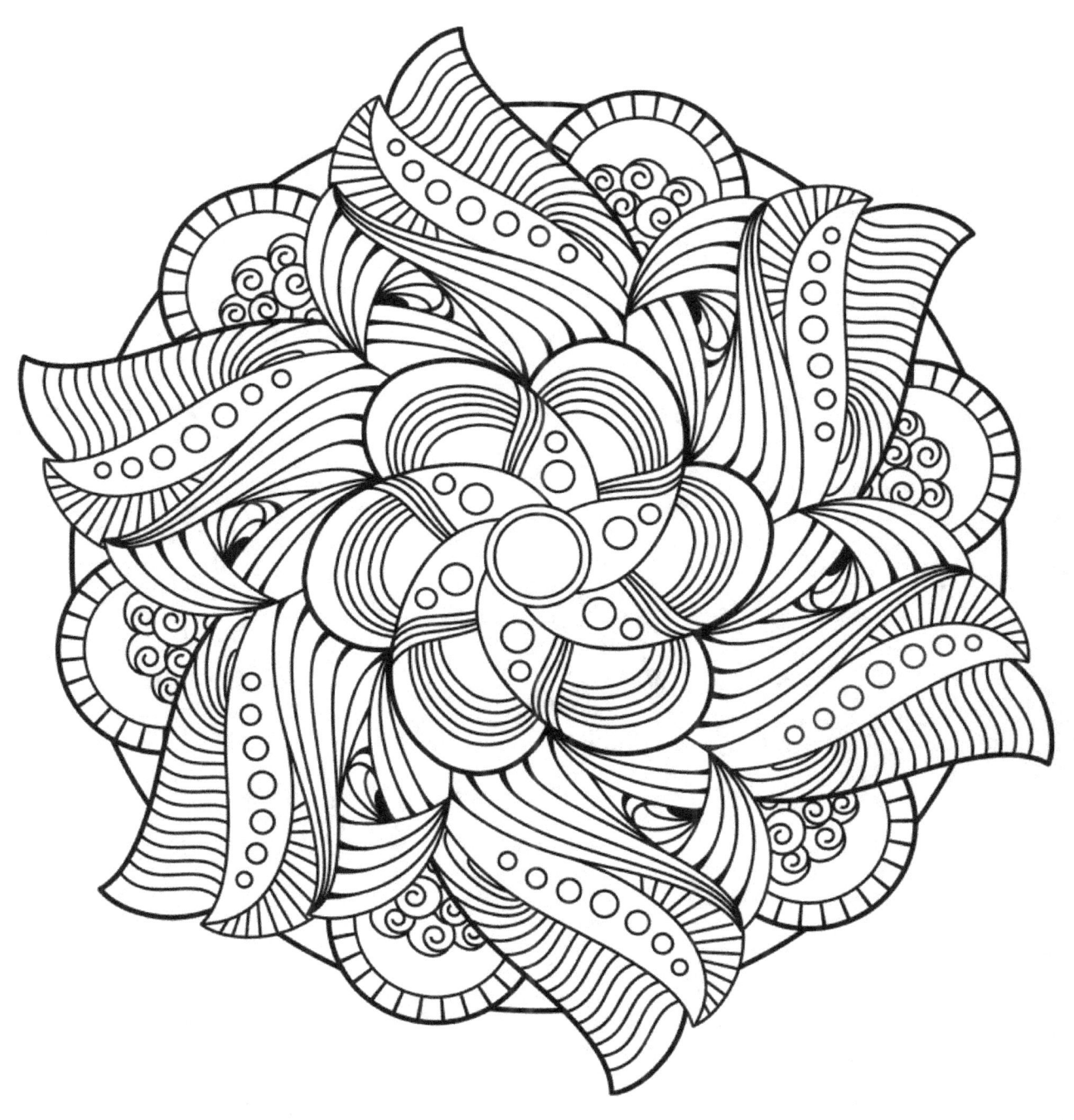

in confusion finds peace

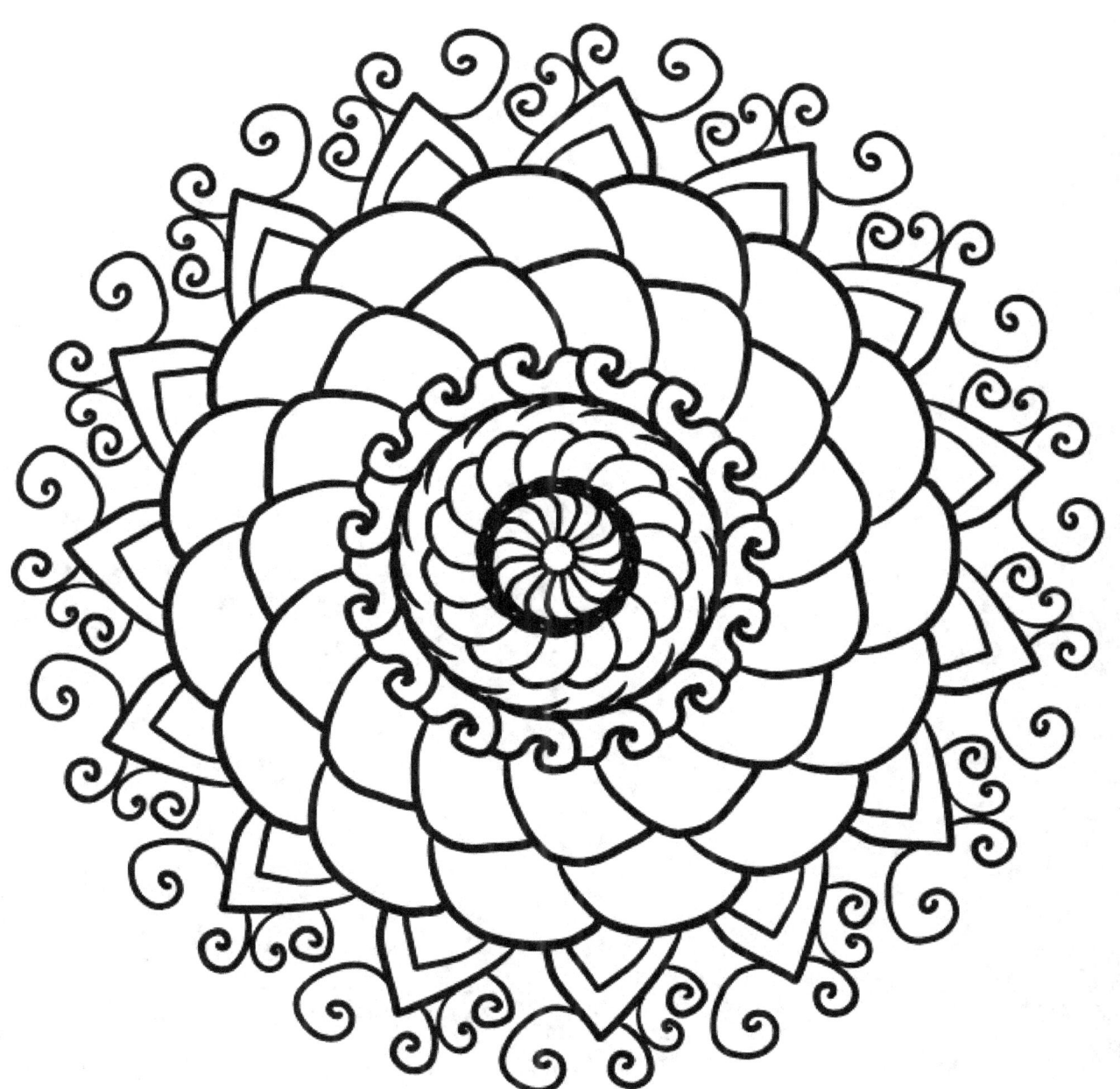

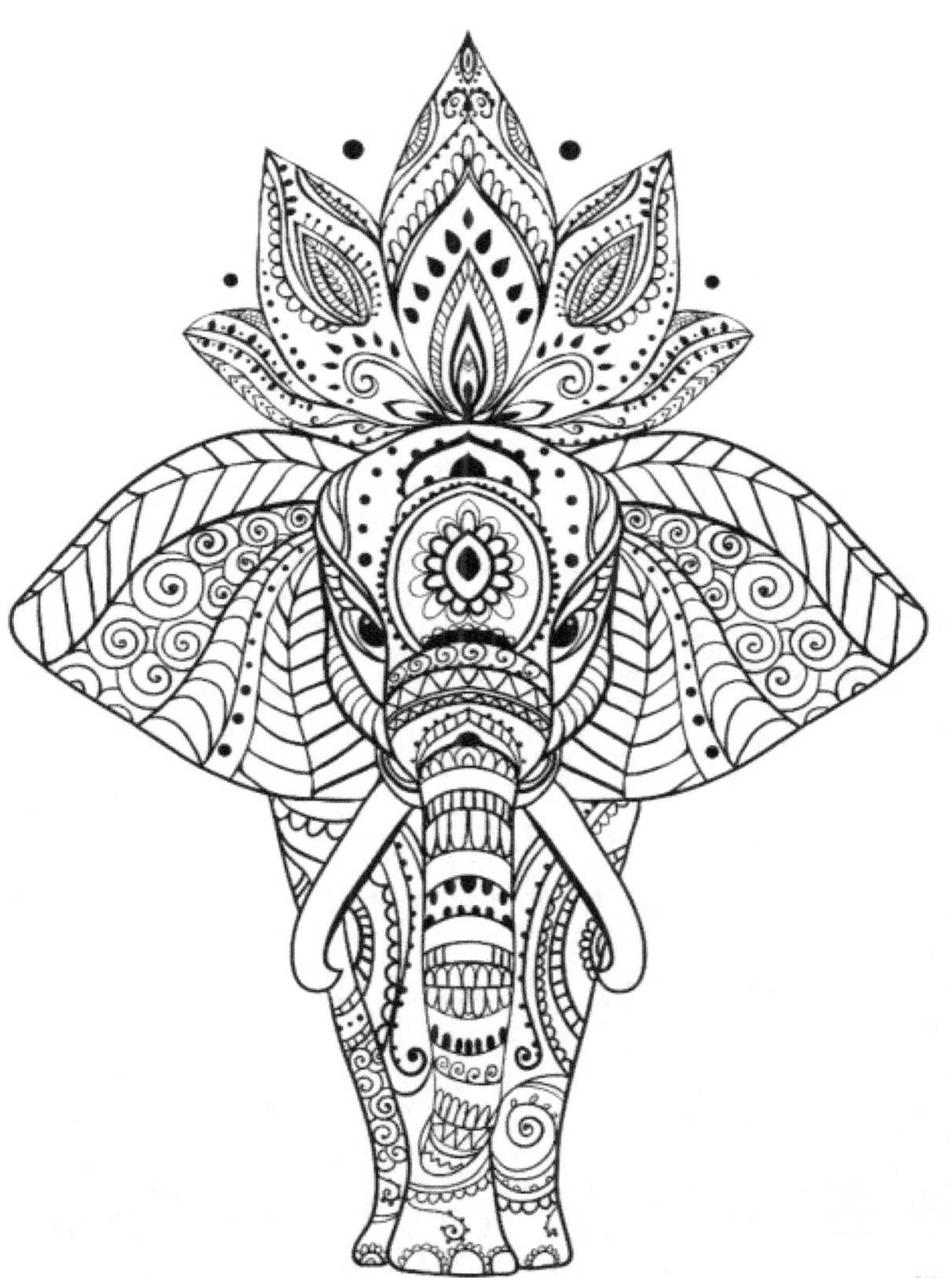

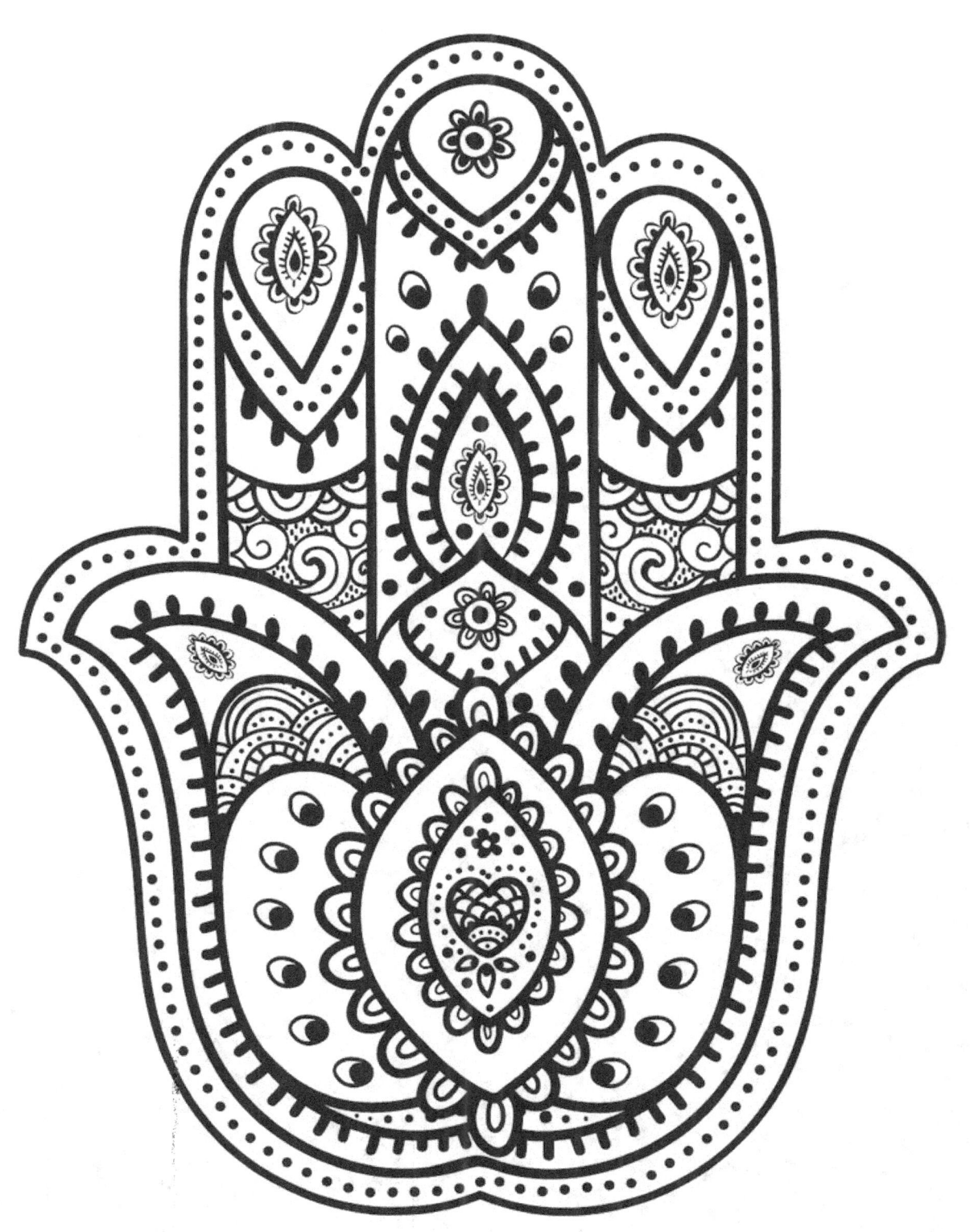

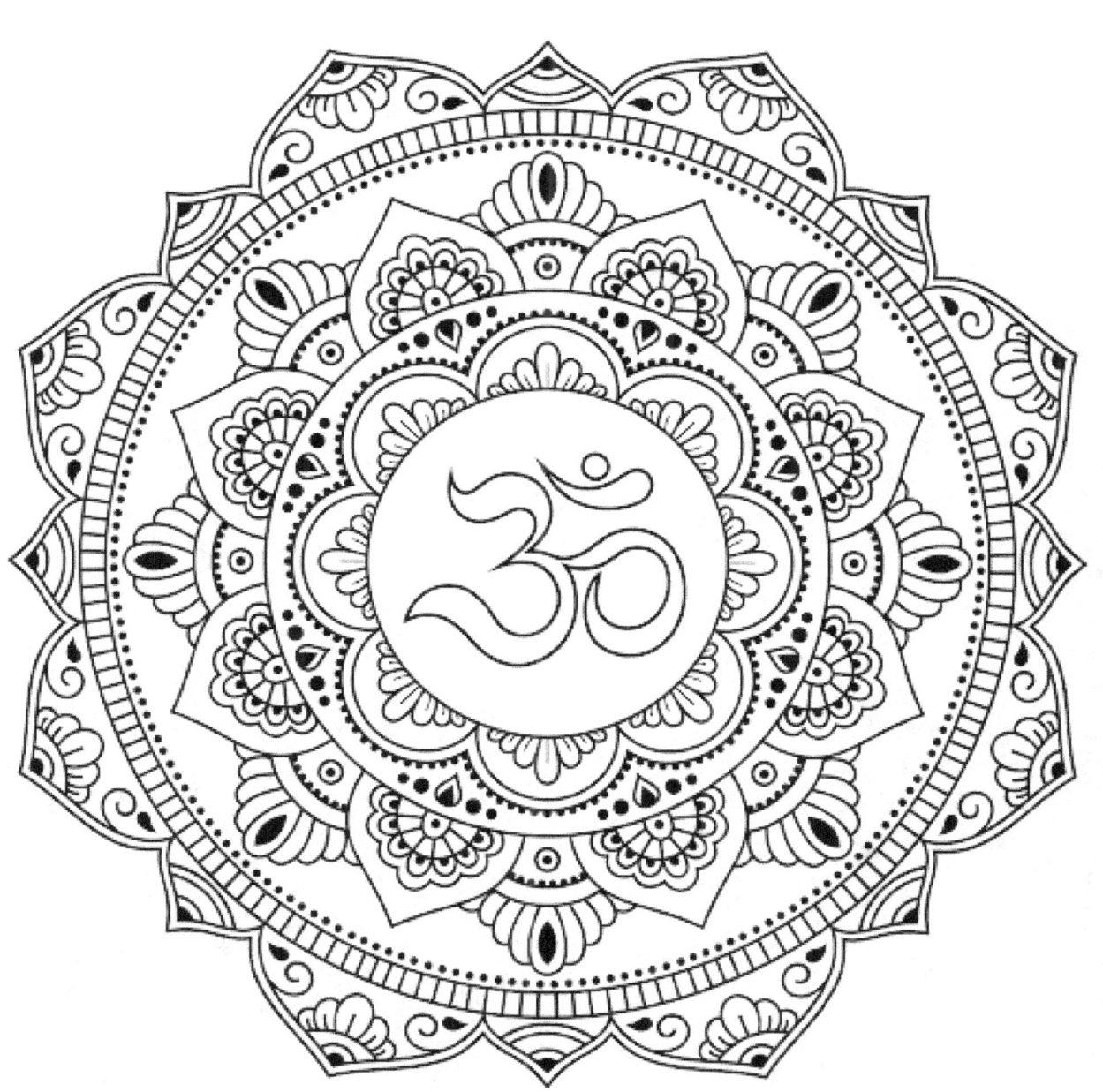

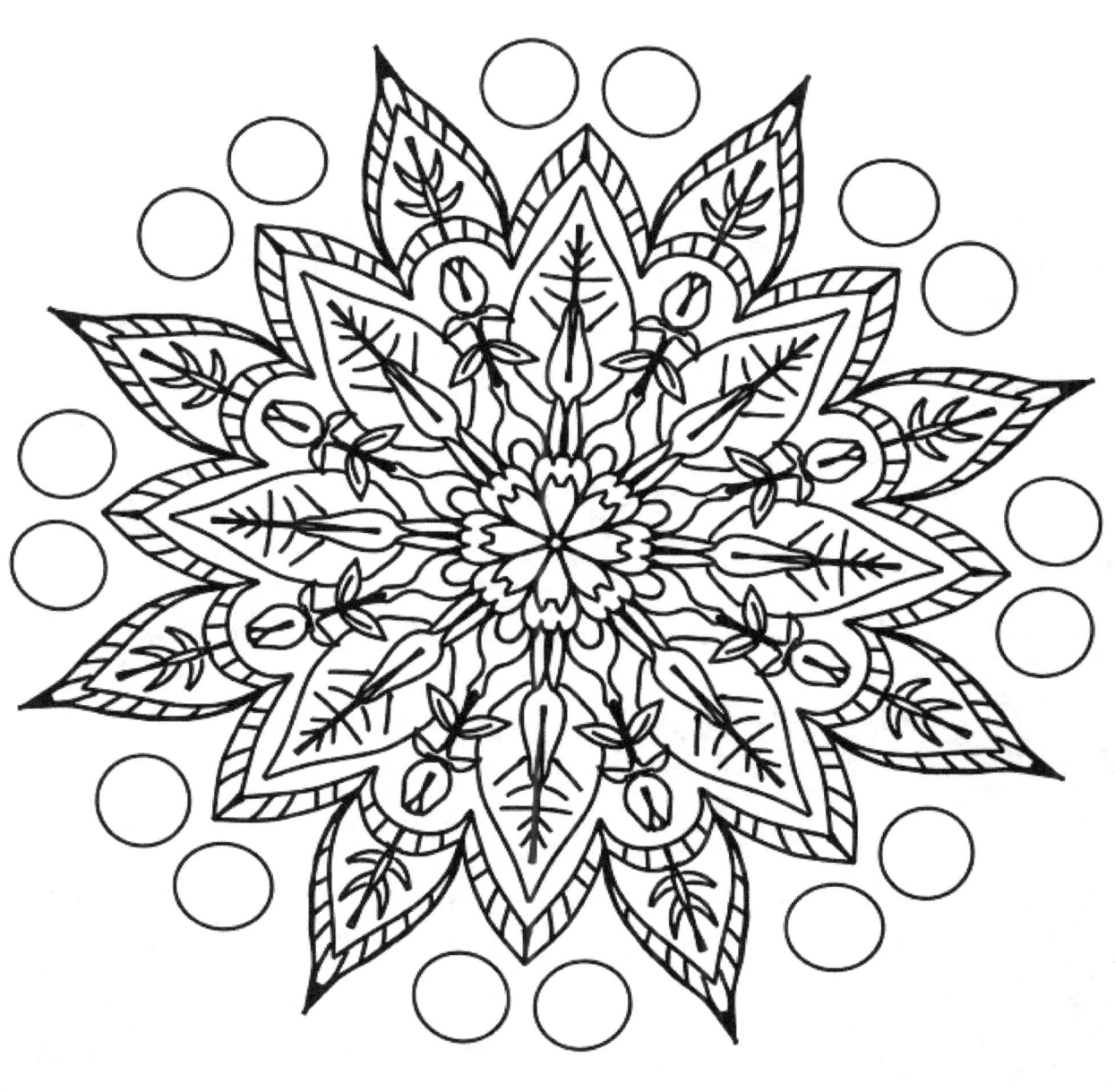

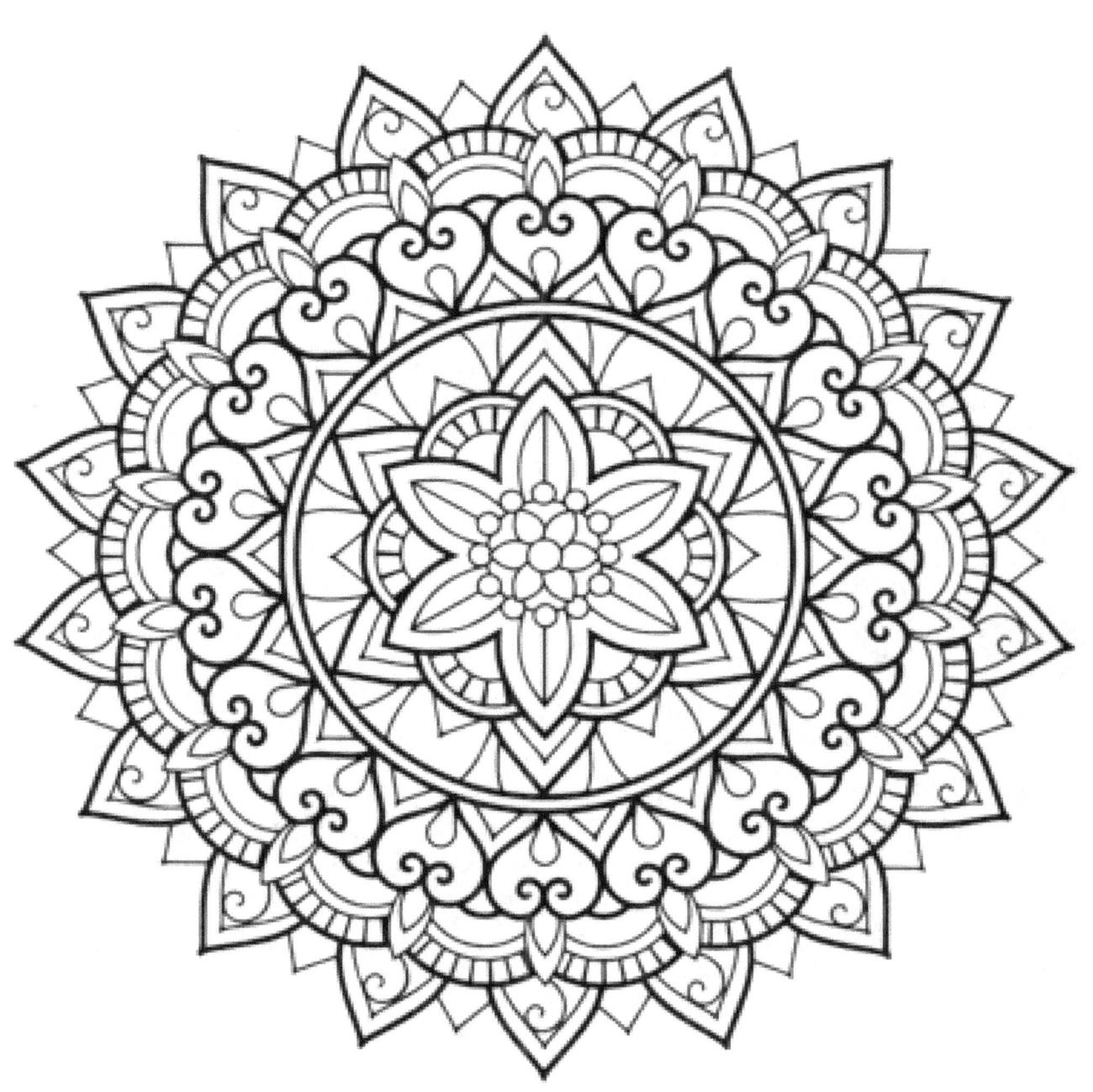

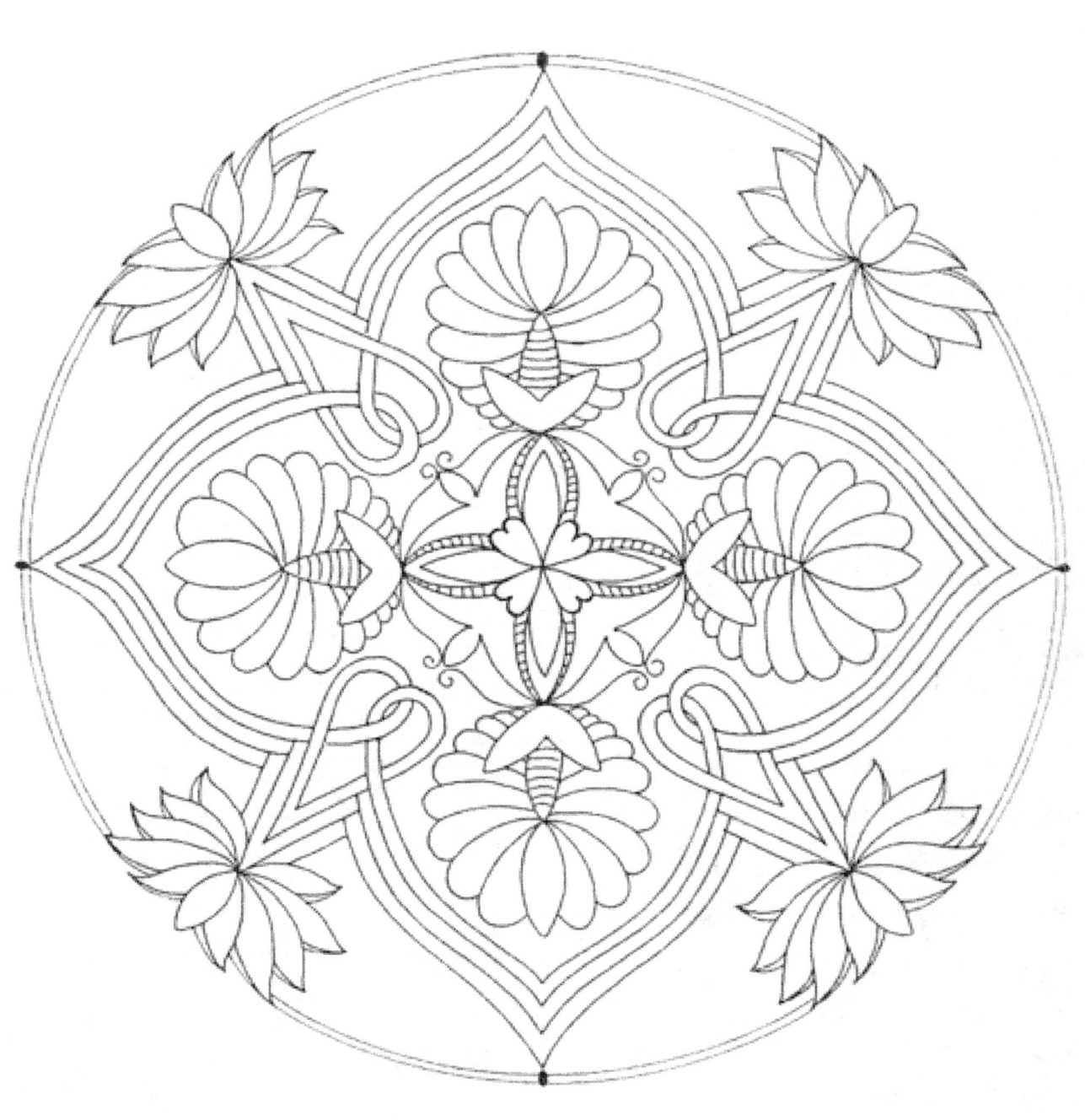

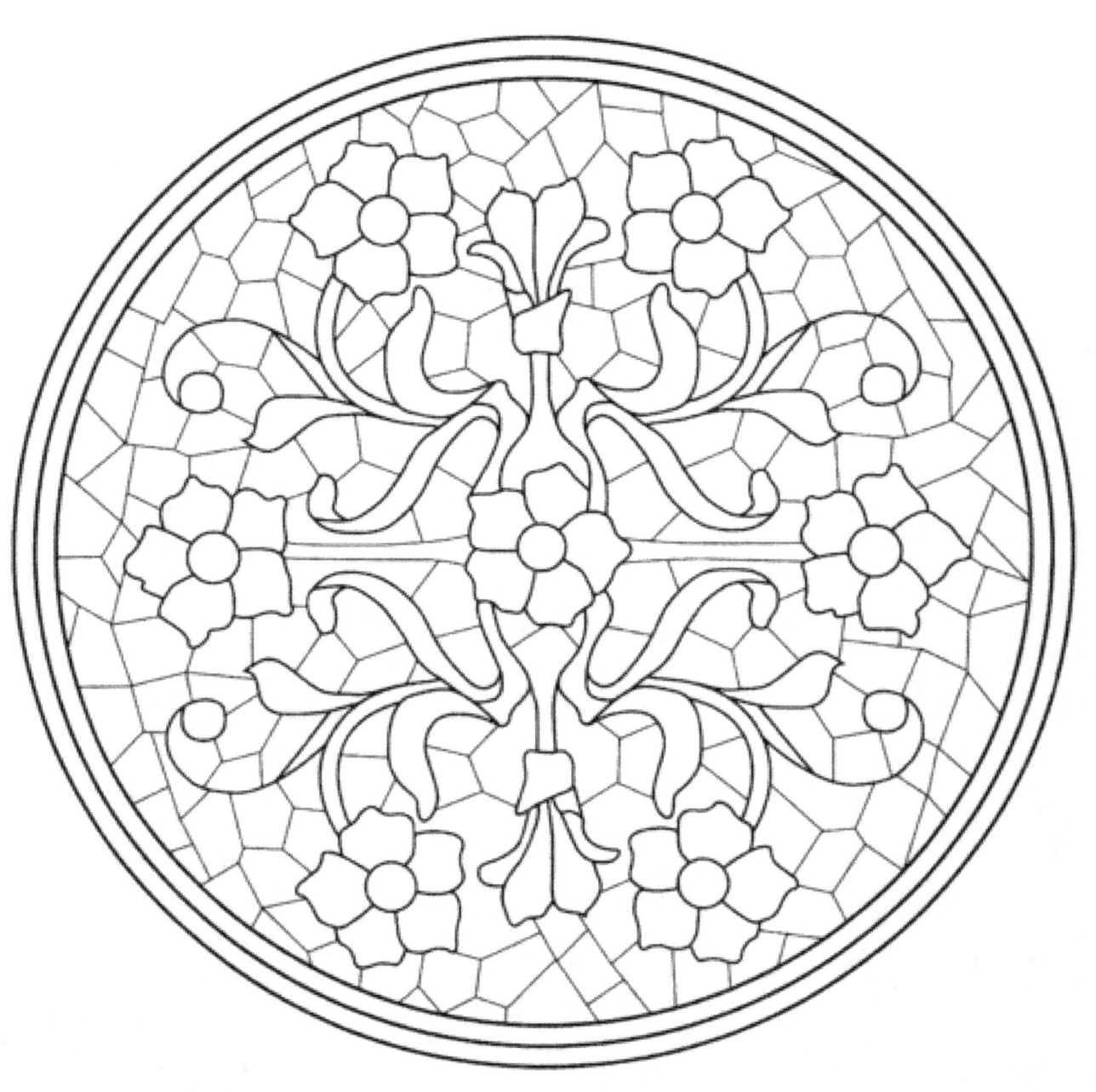

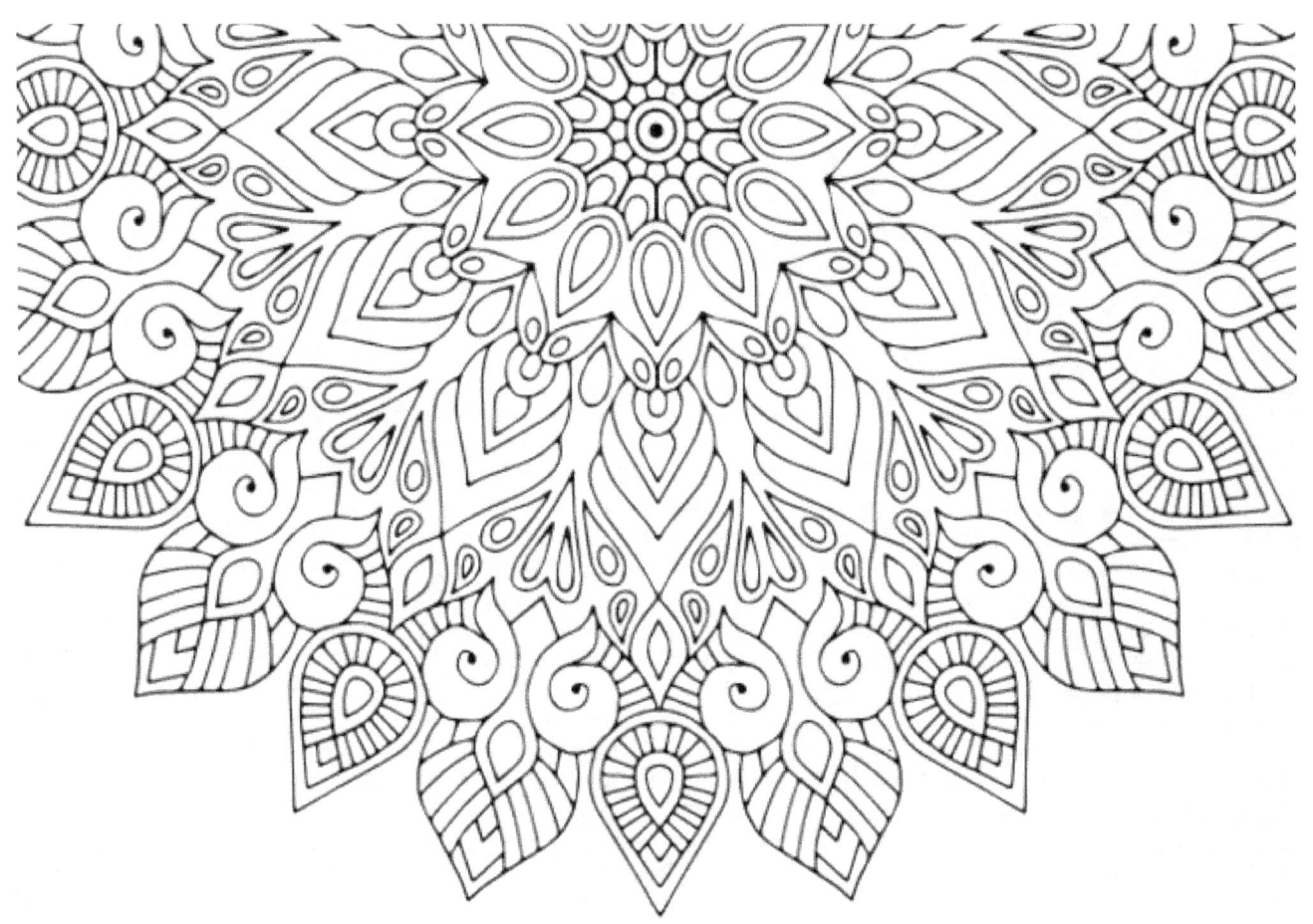

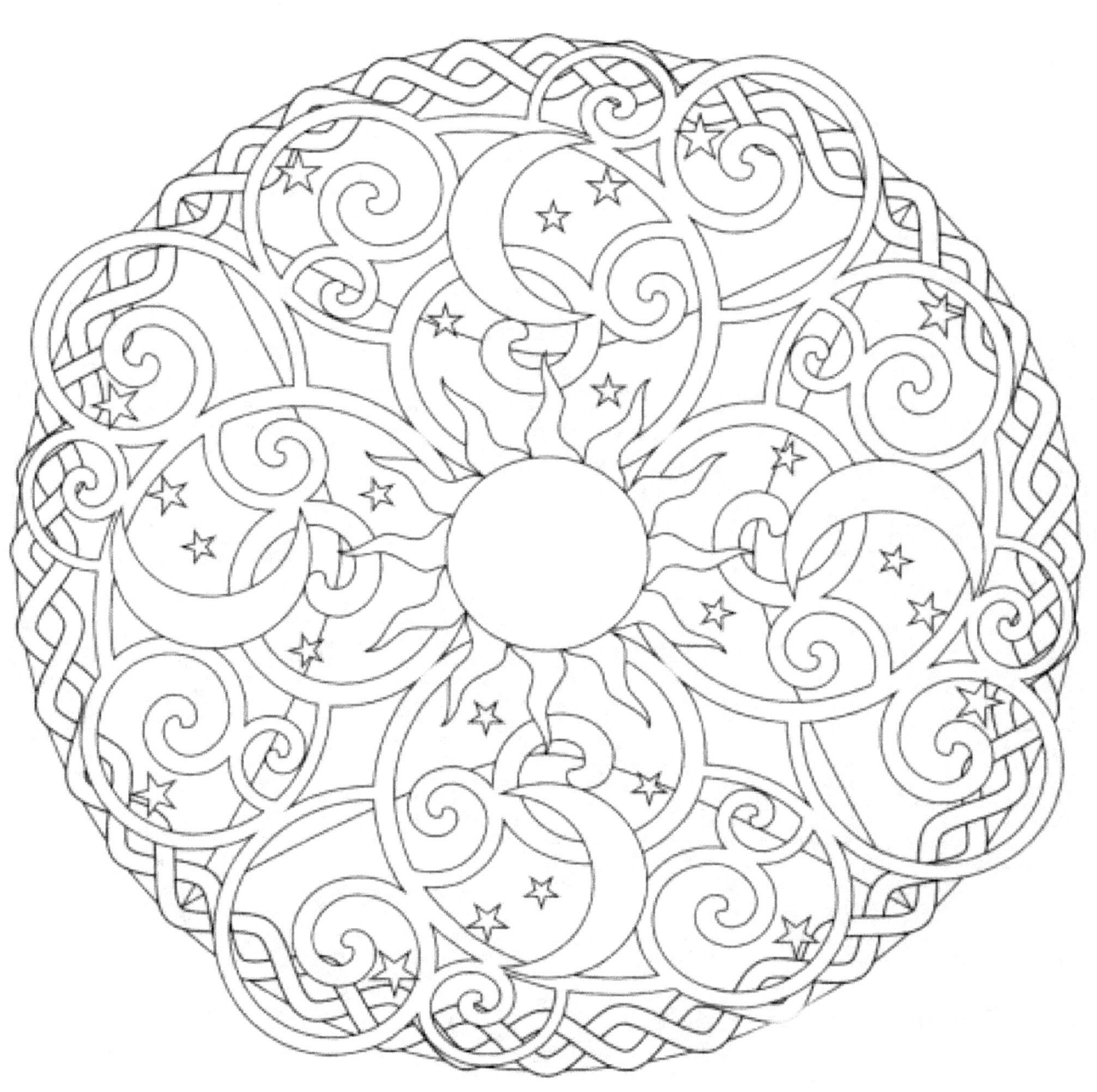

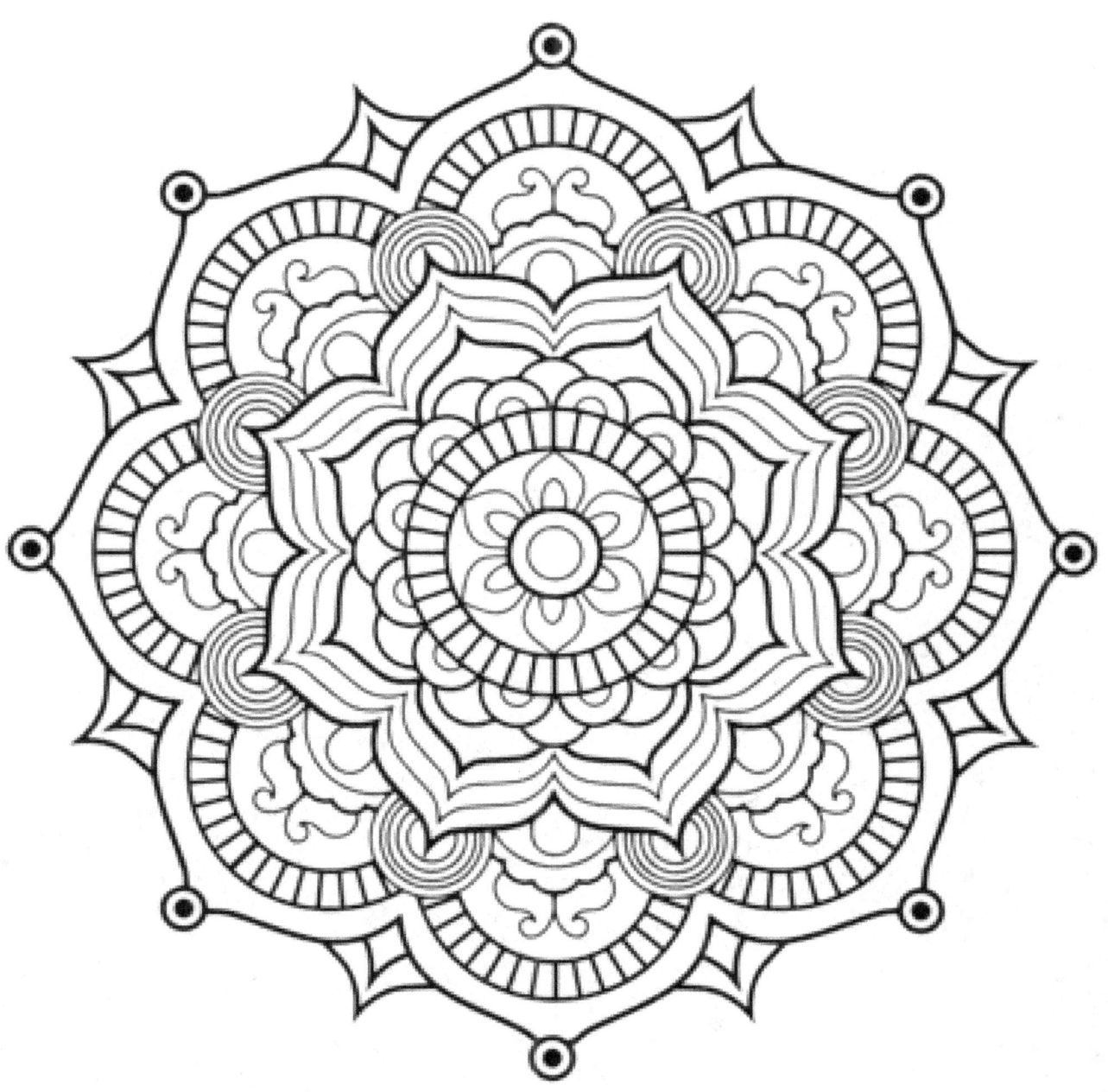

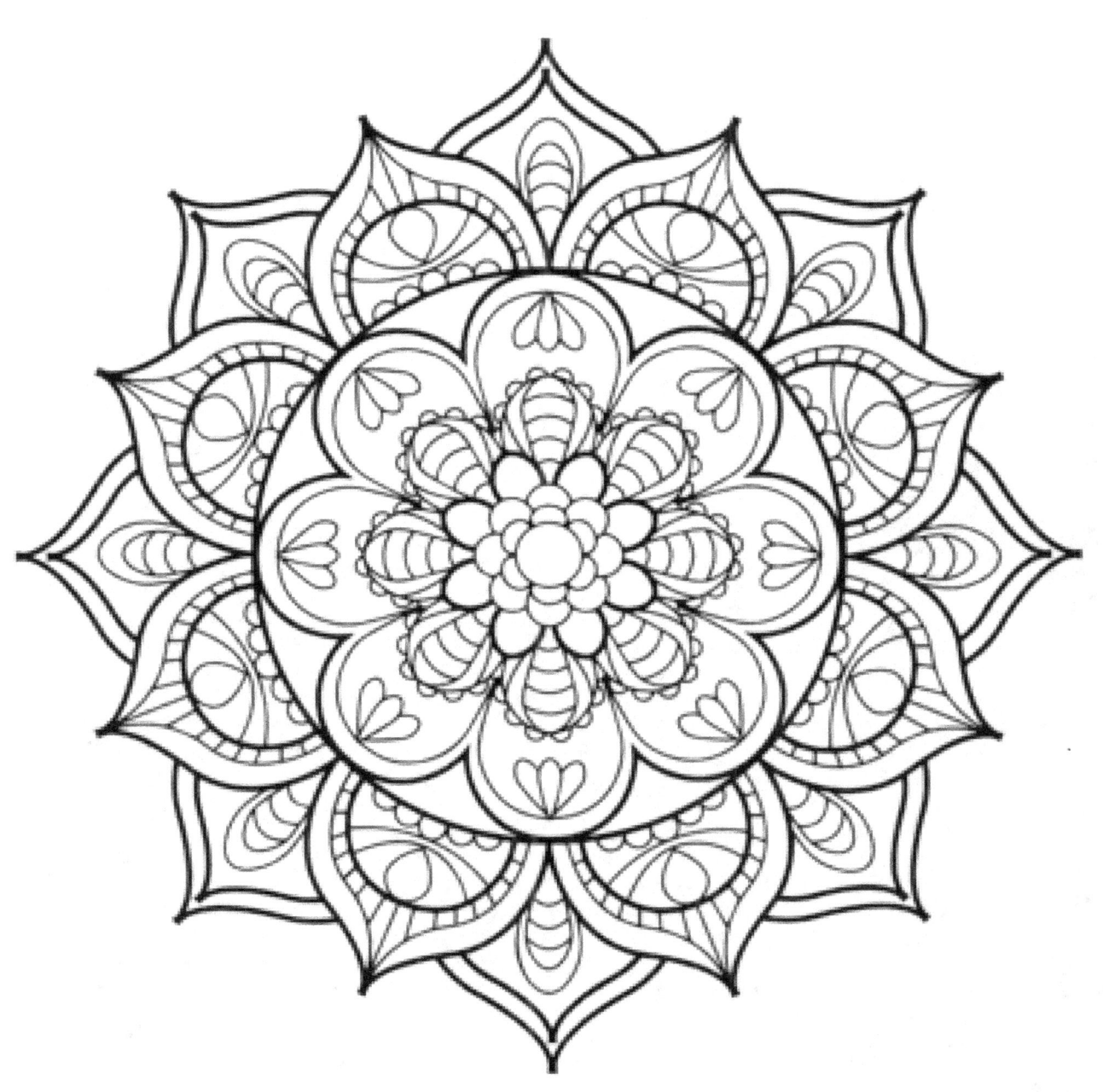

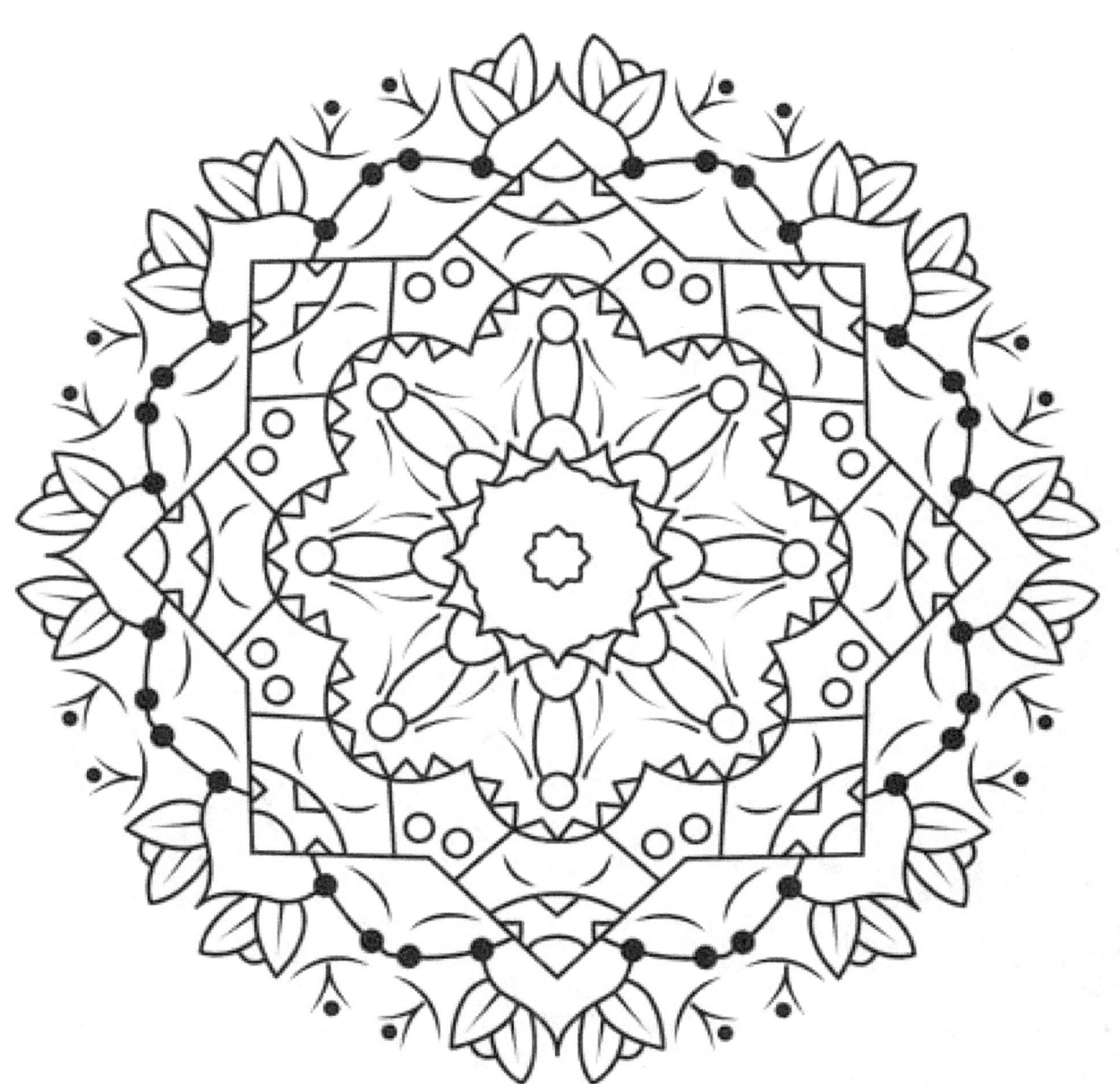

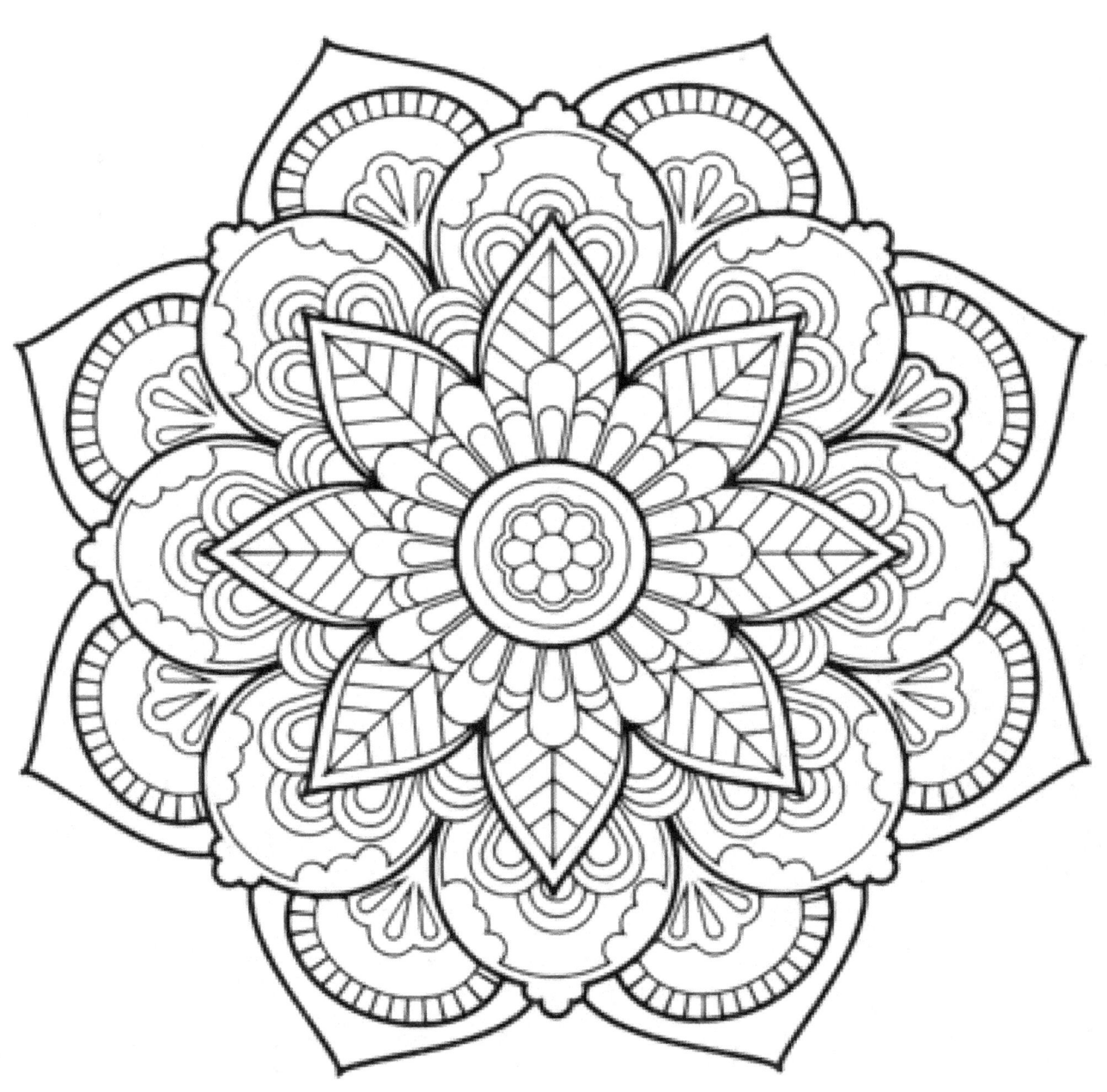

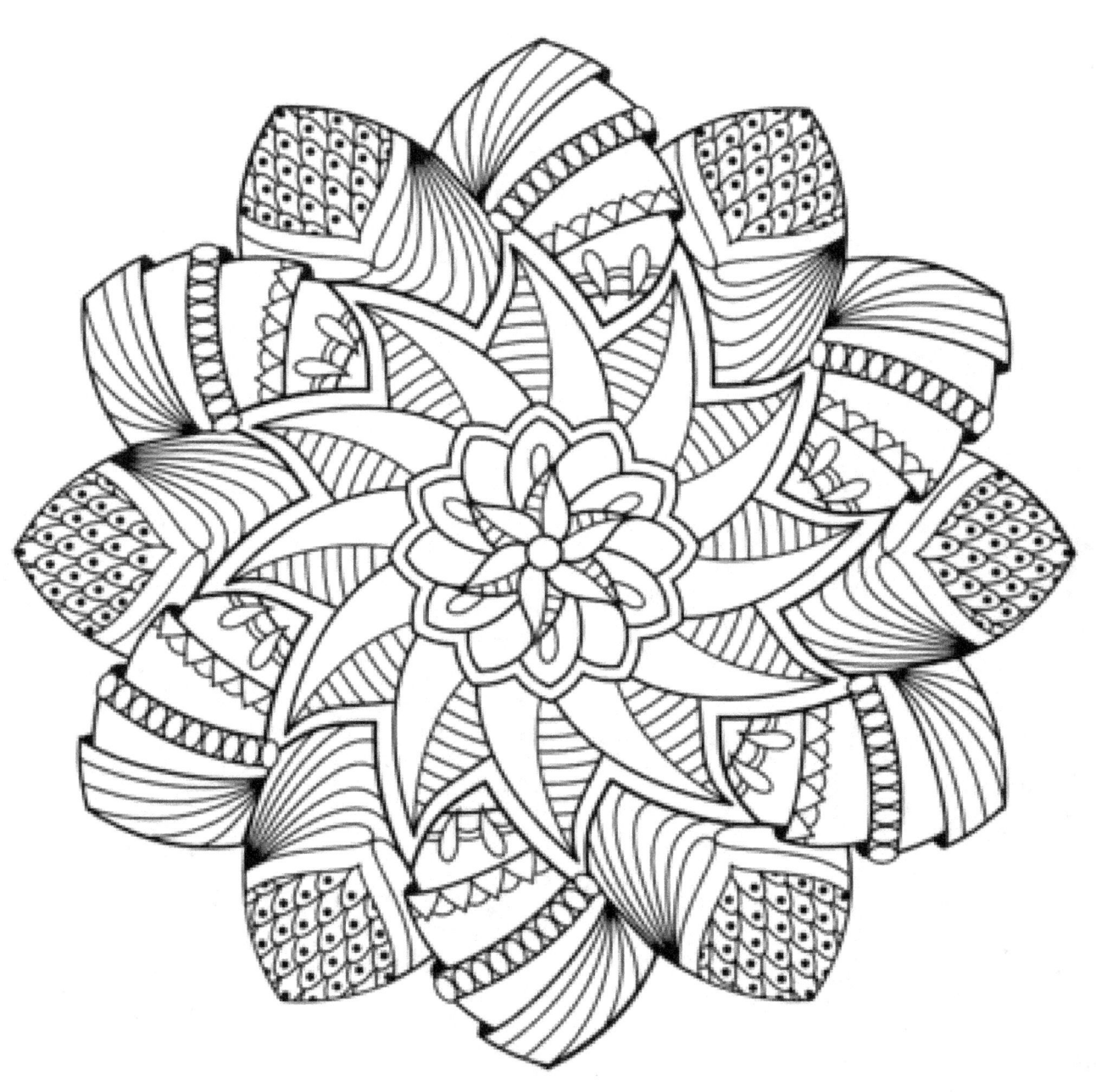

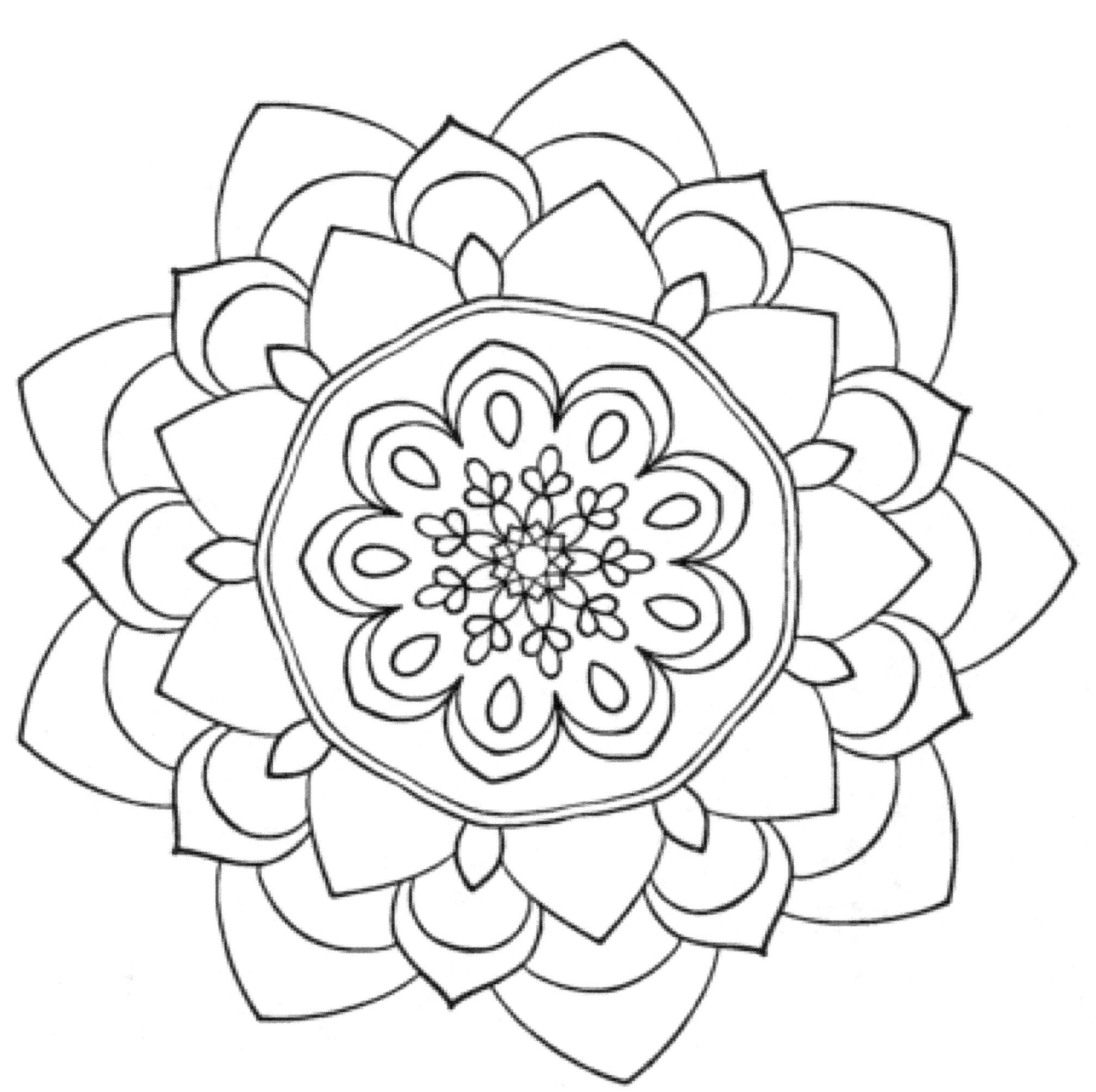

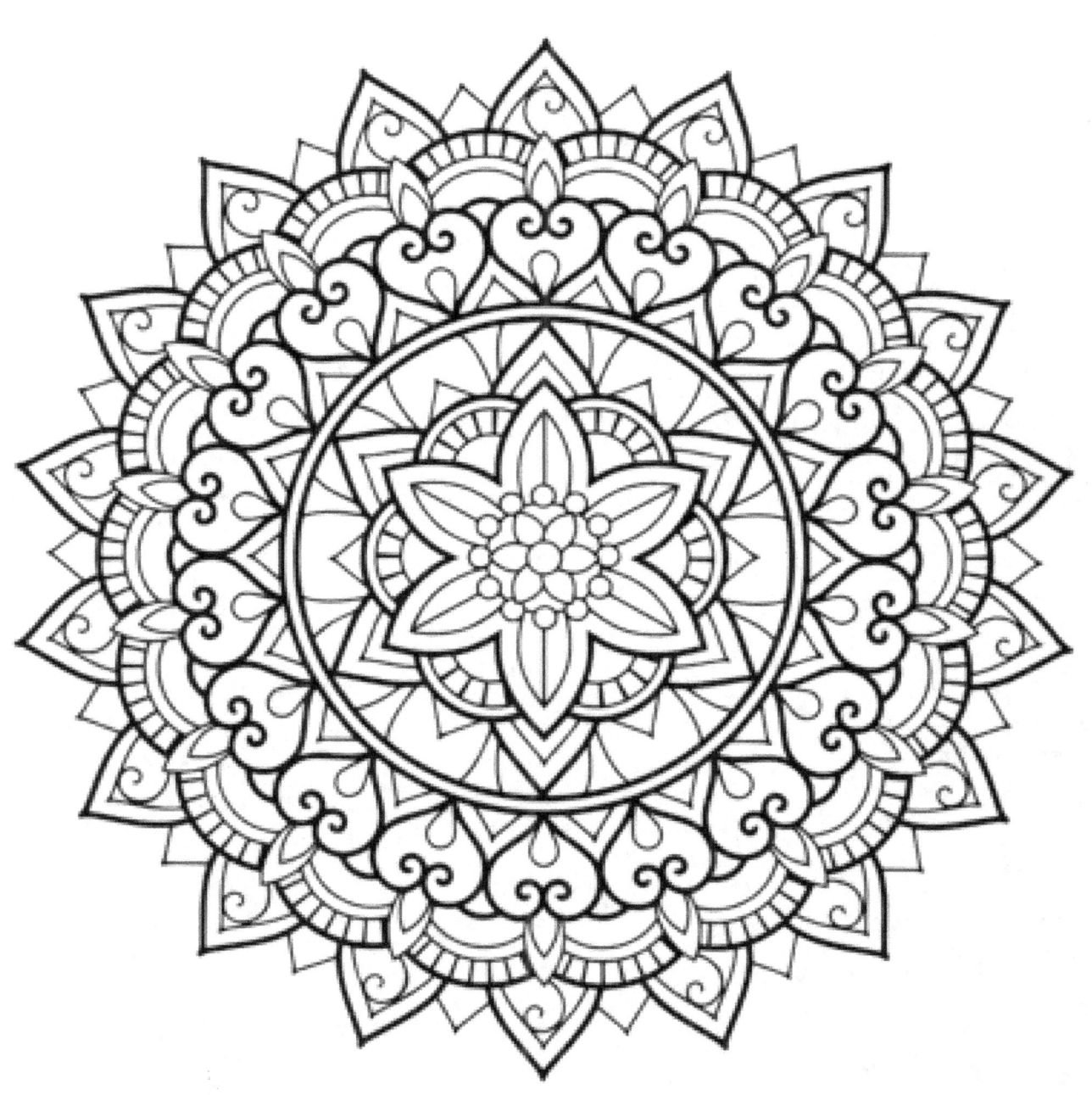

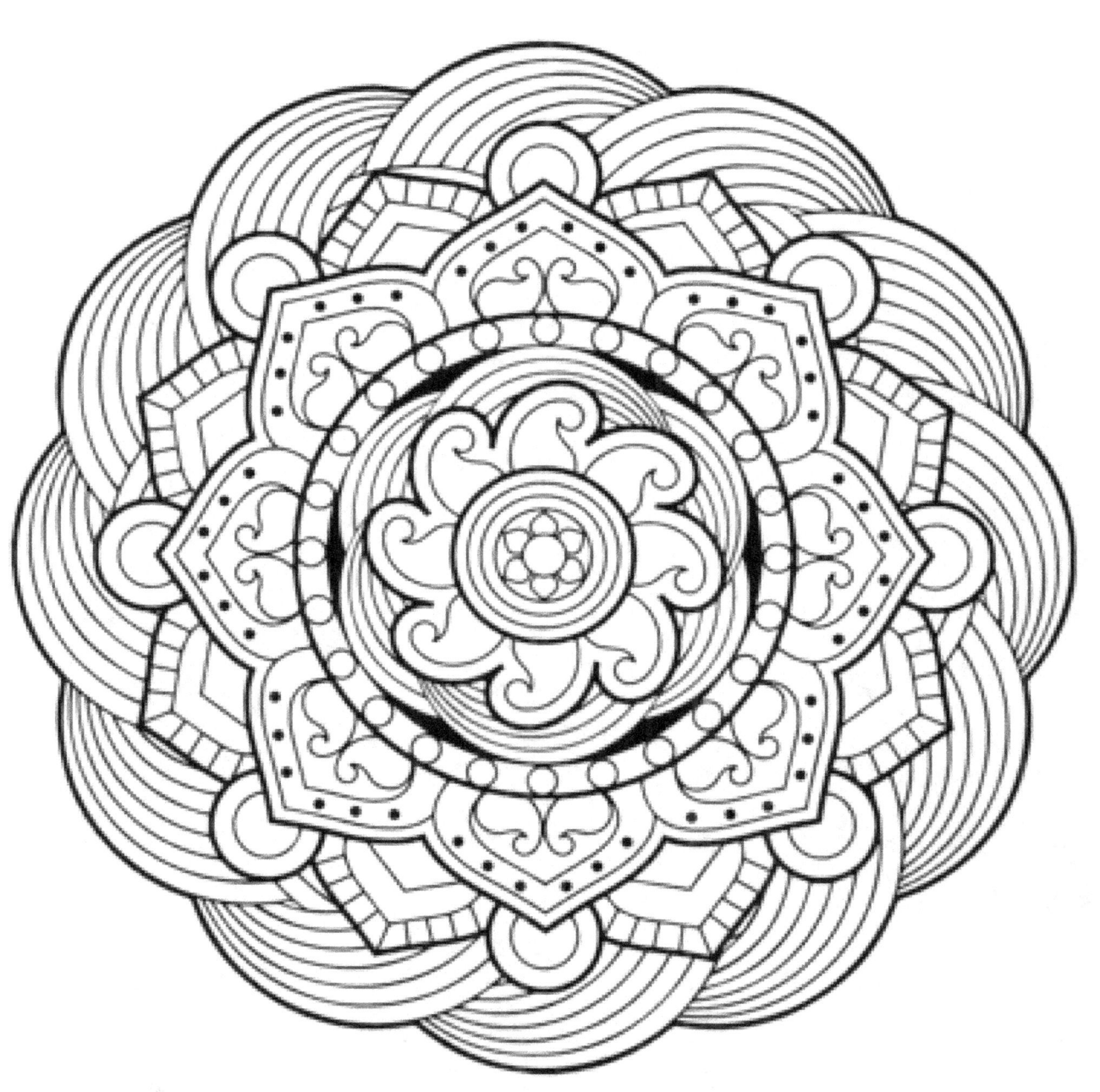

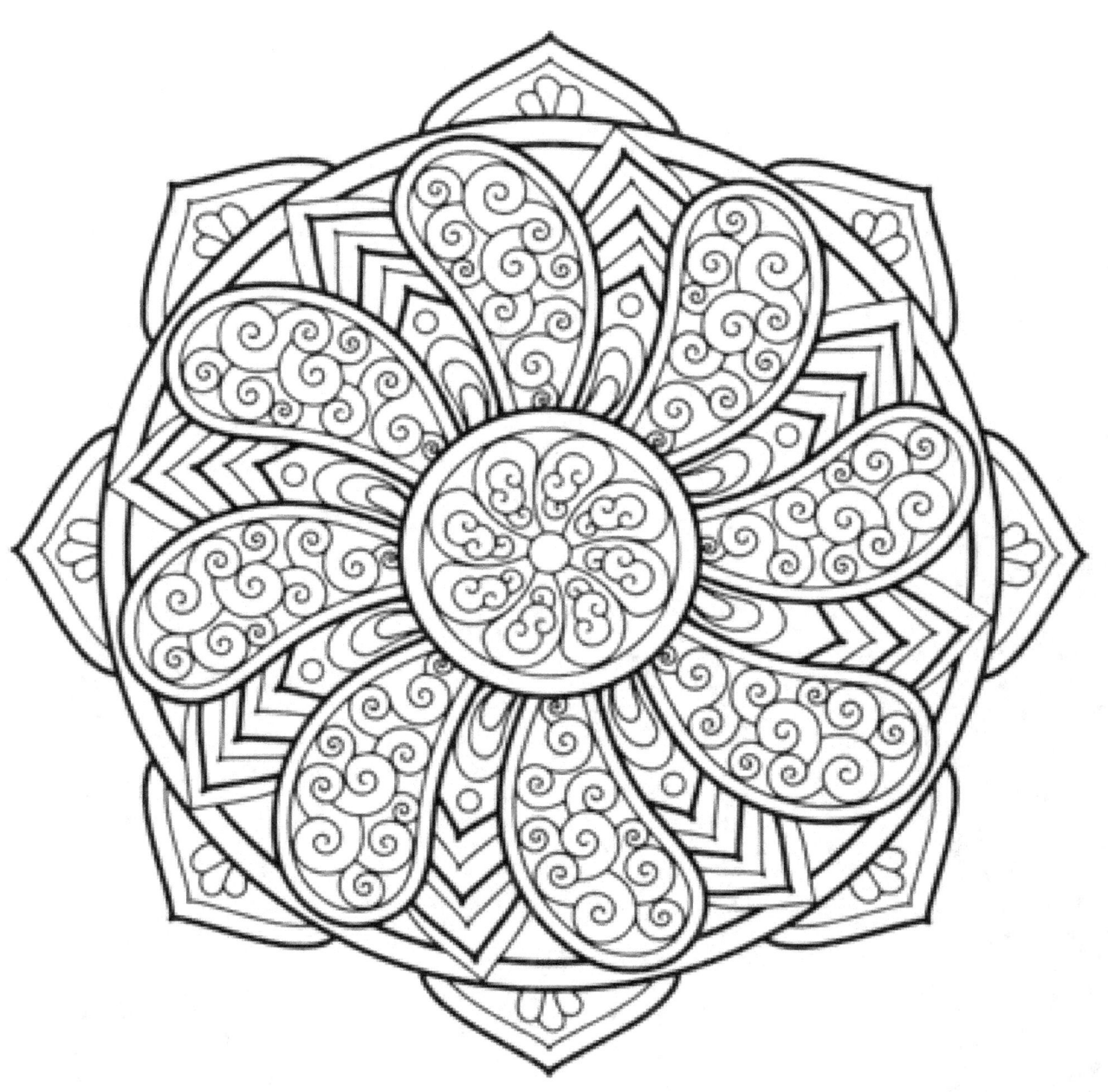

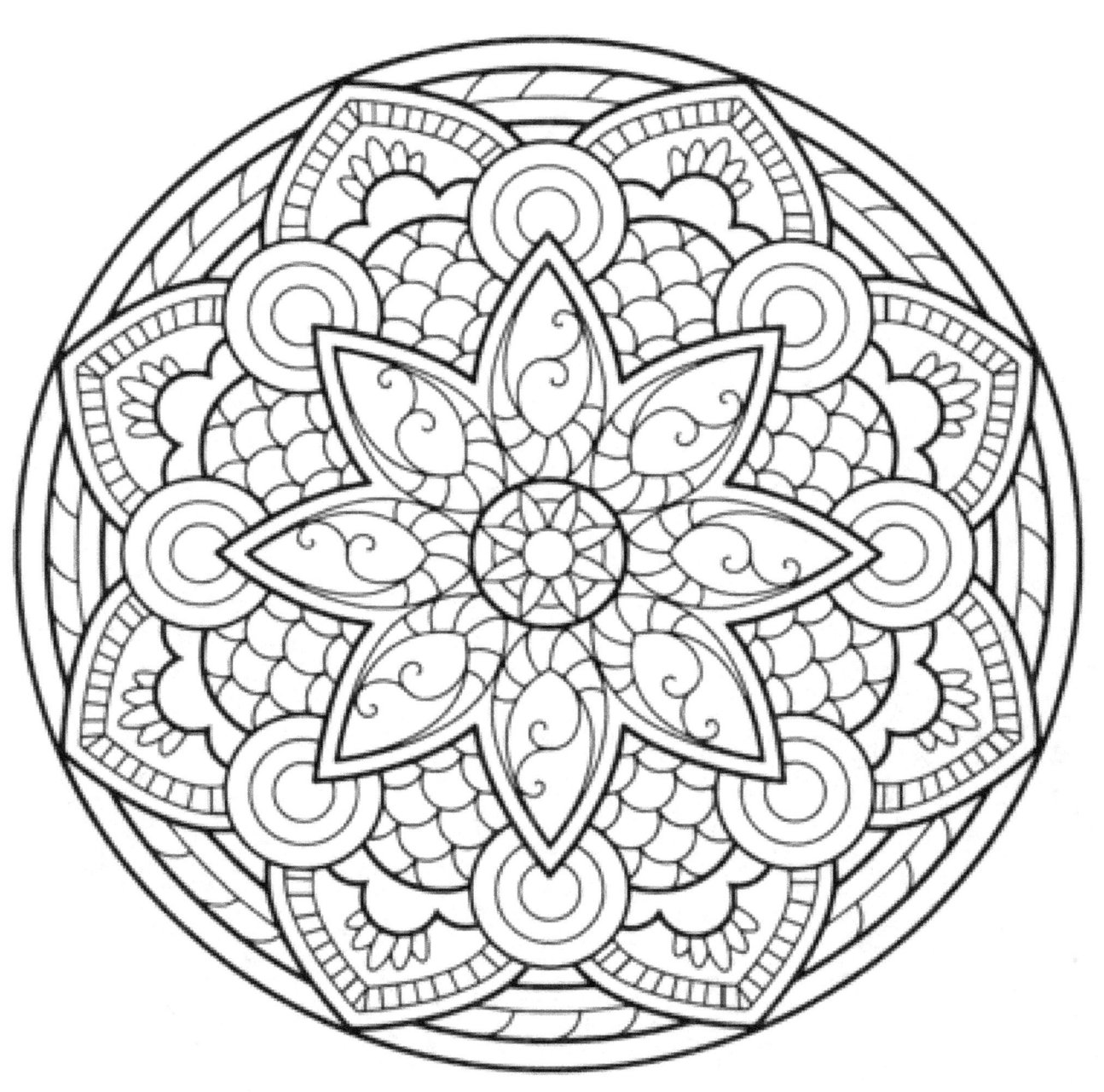

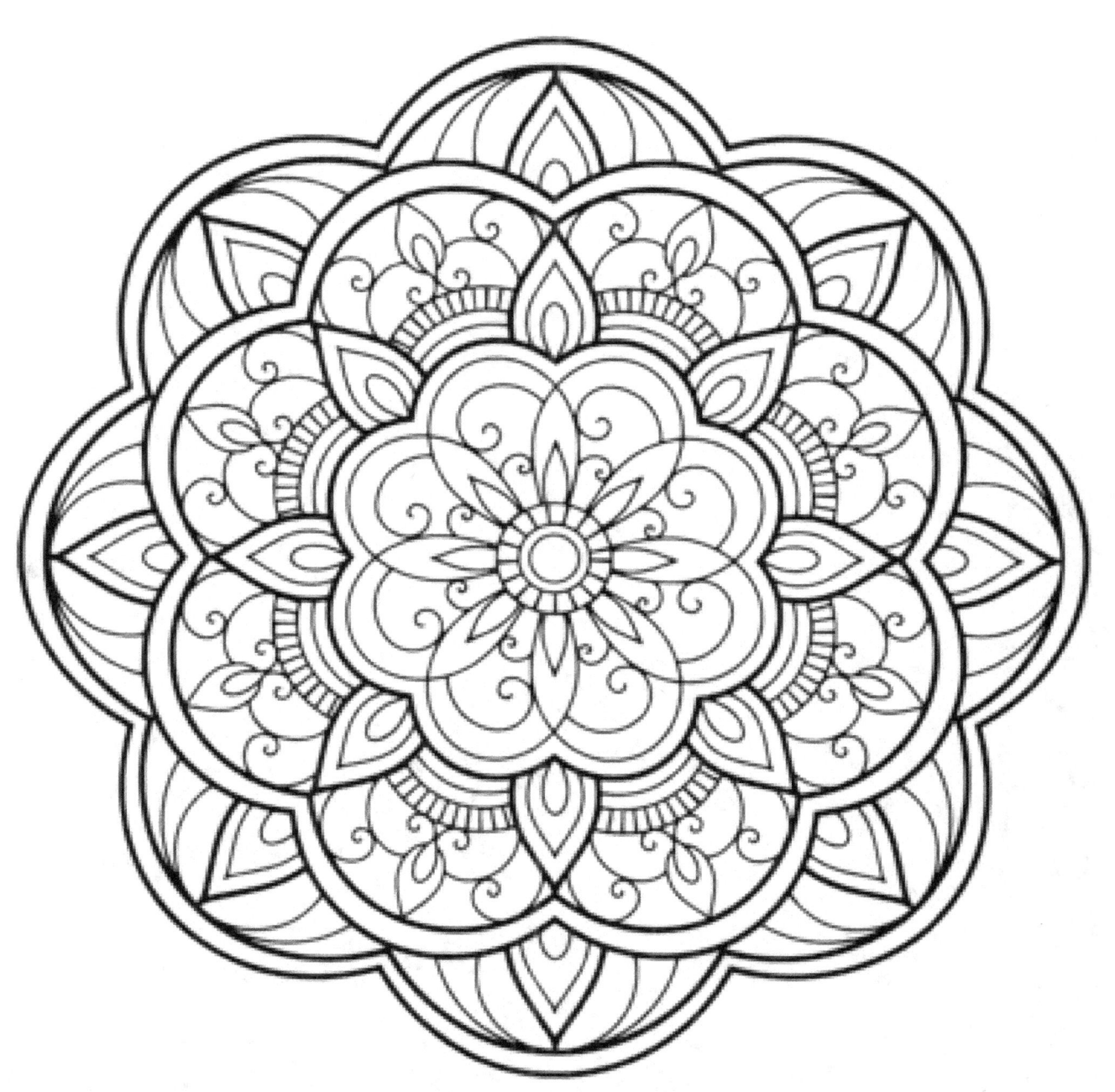

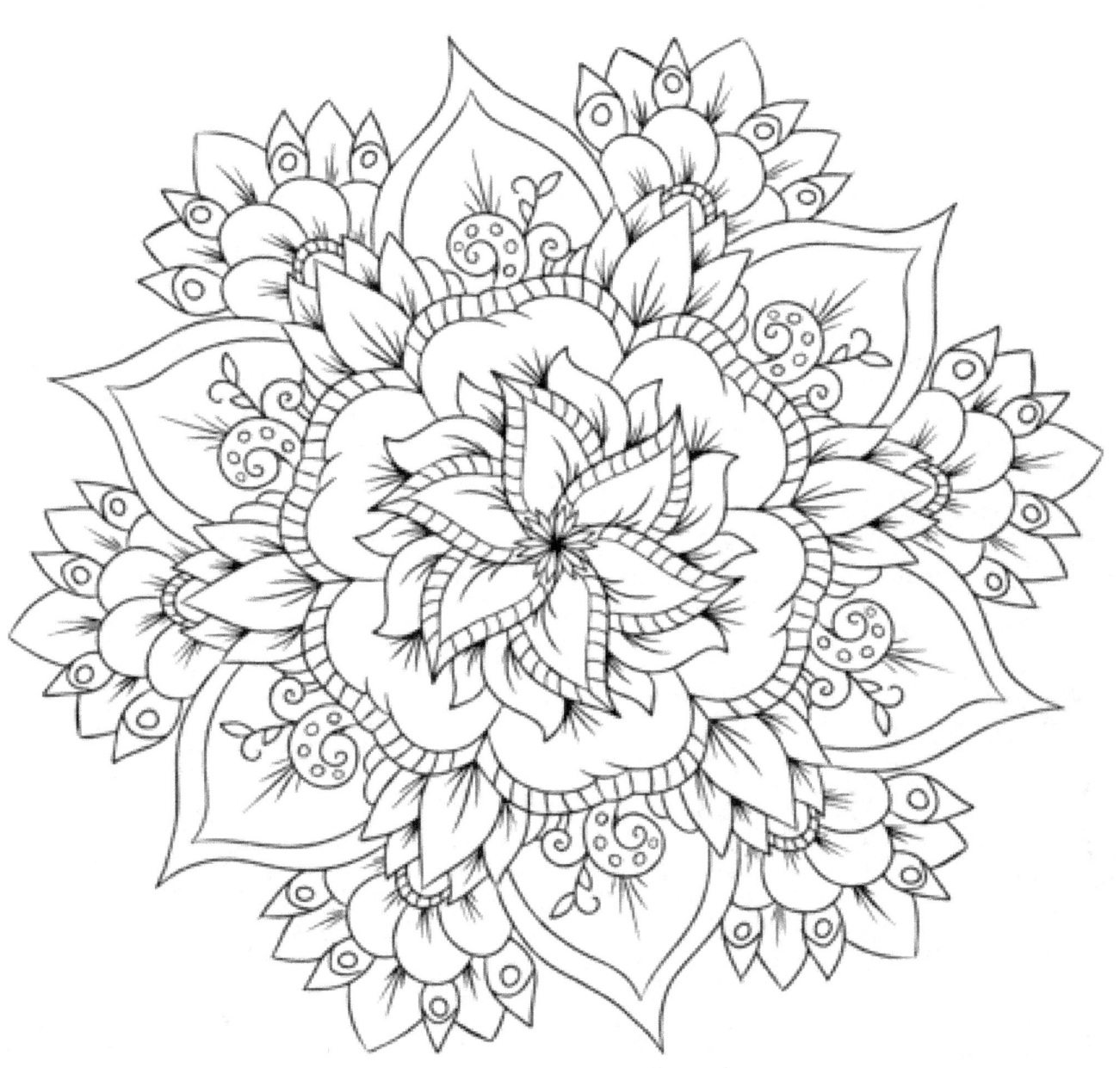

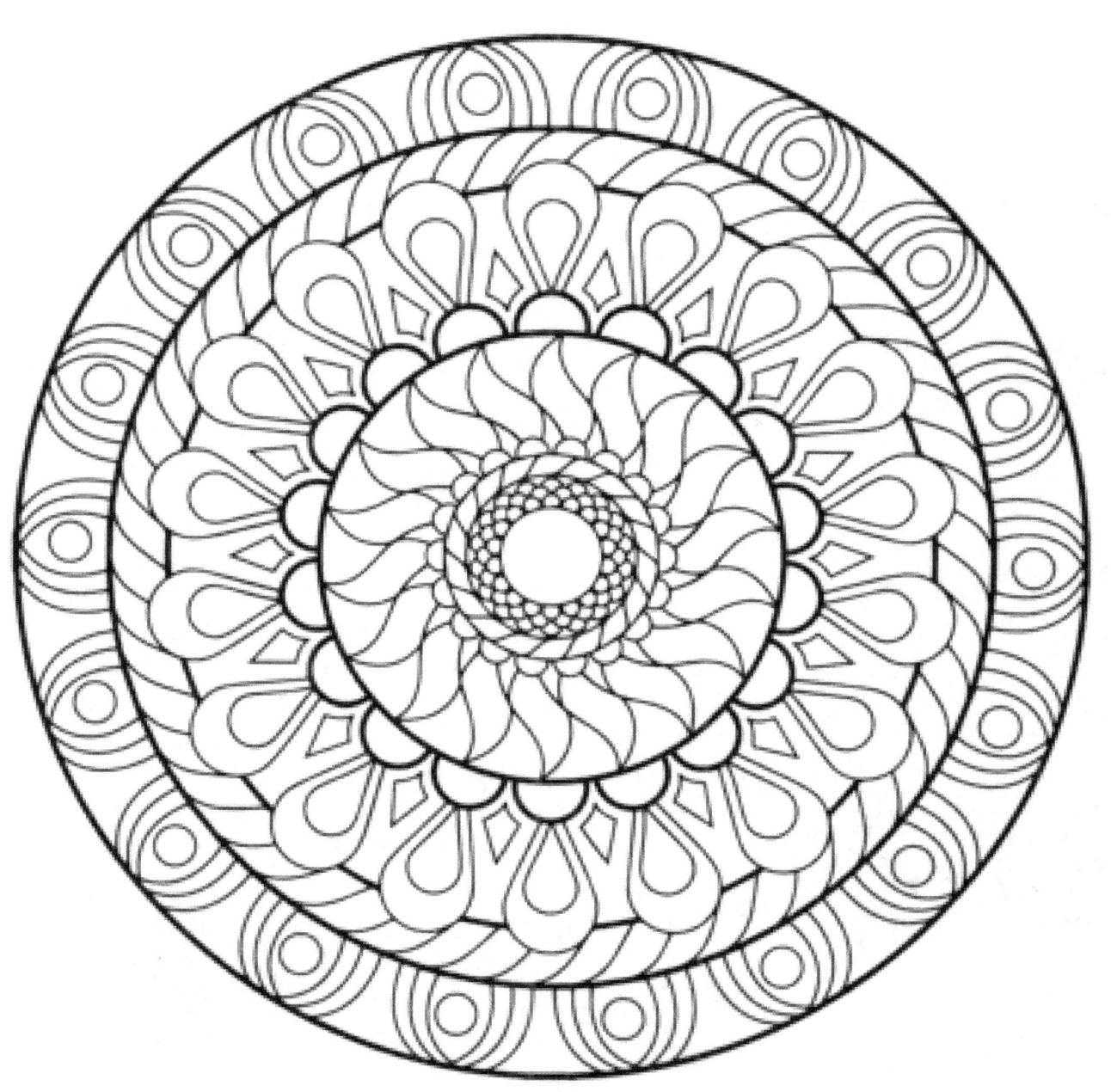

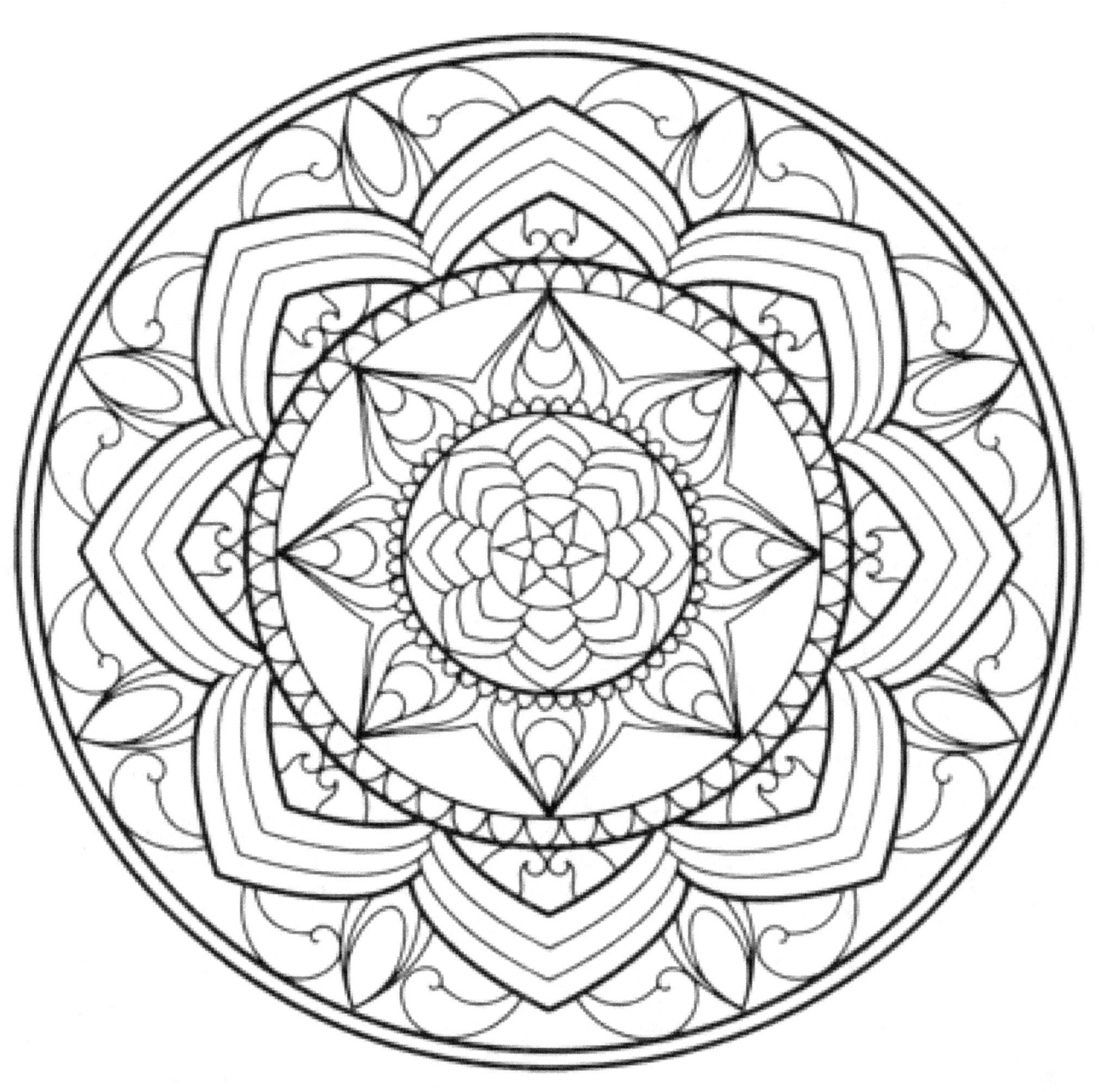

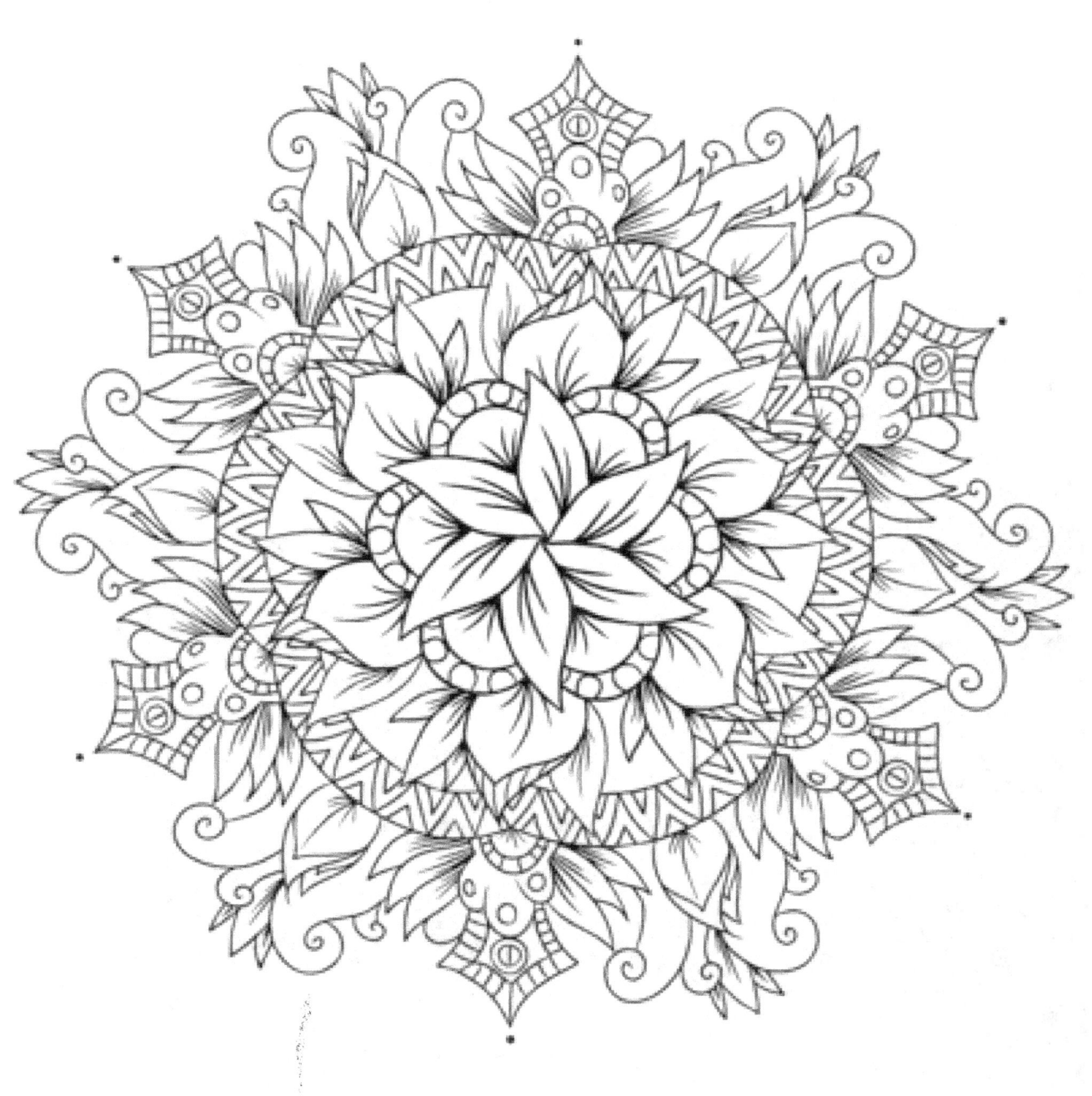

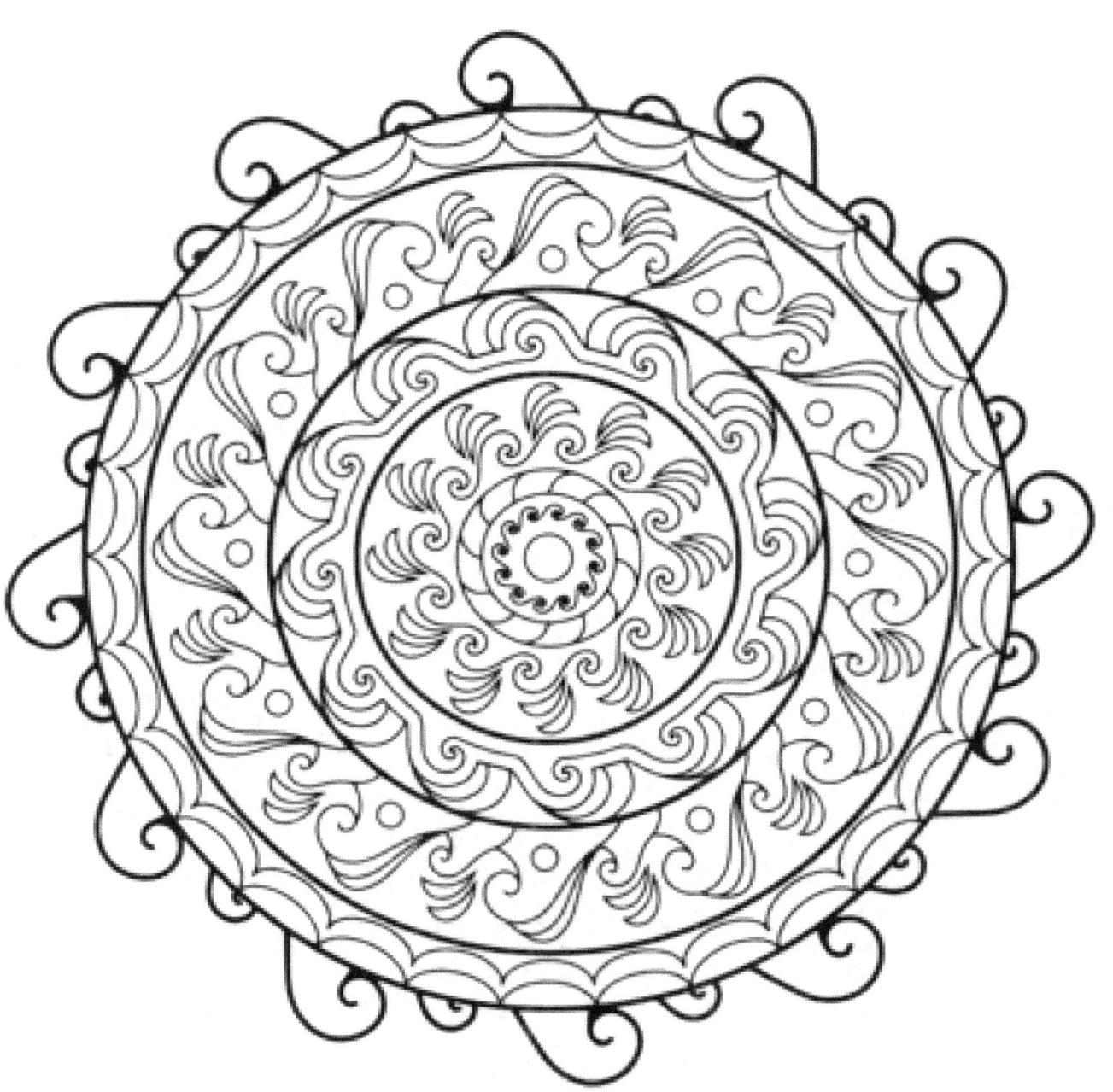

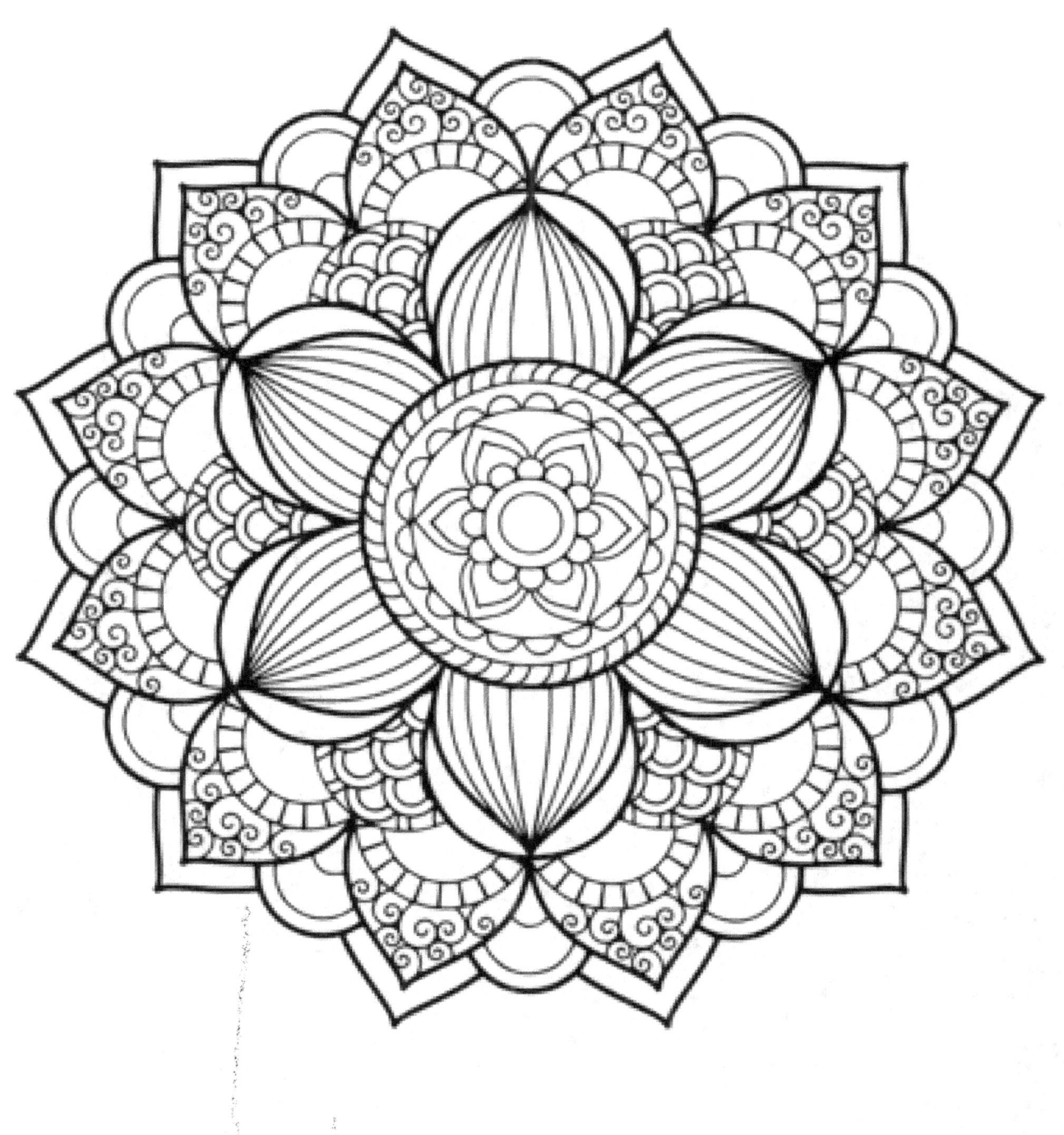

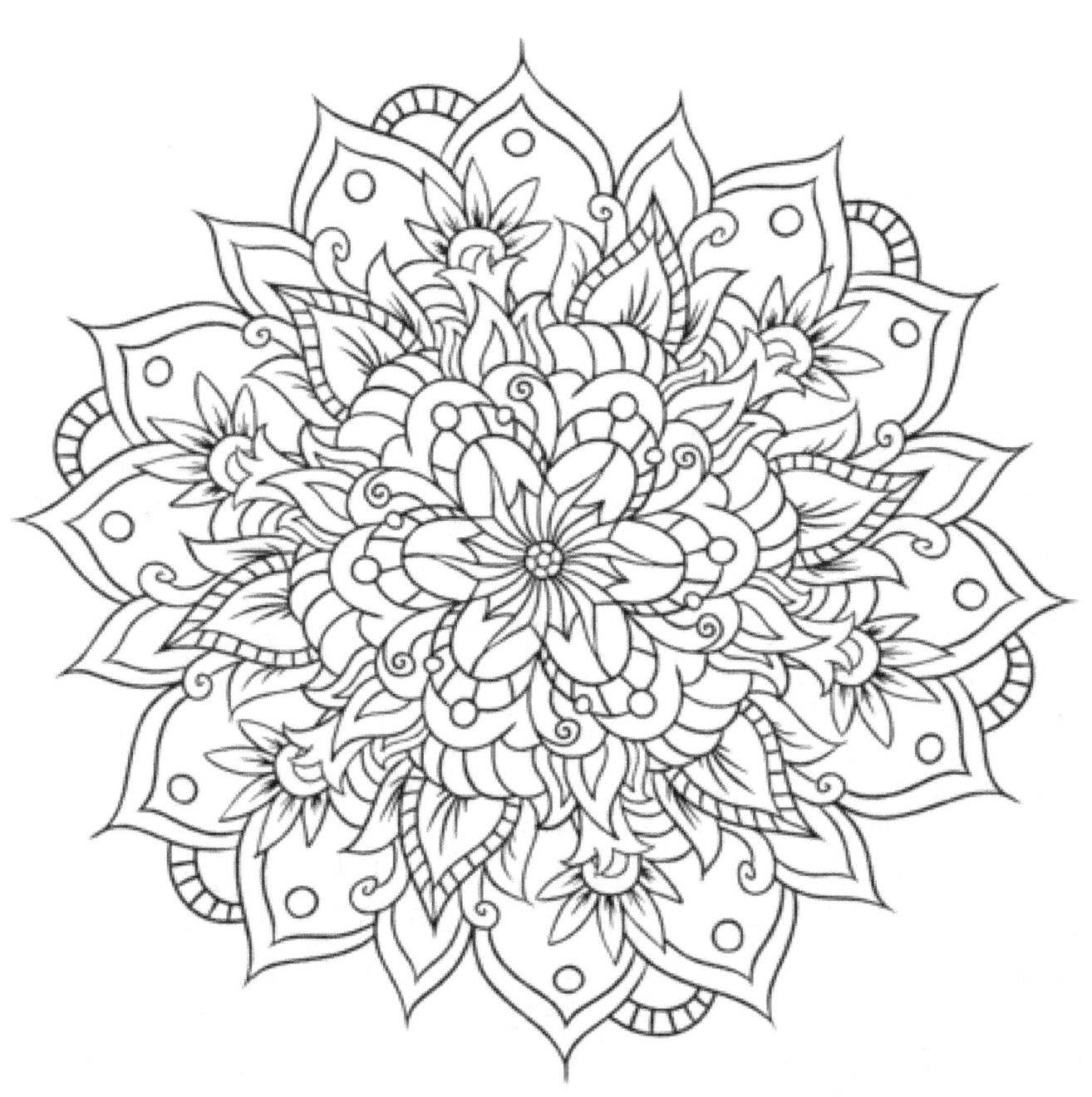

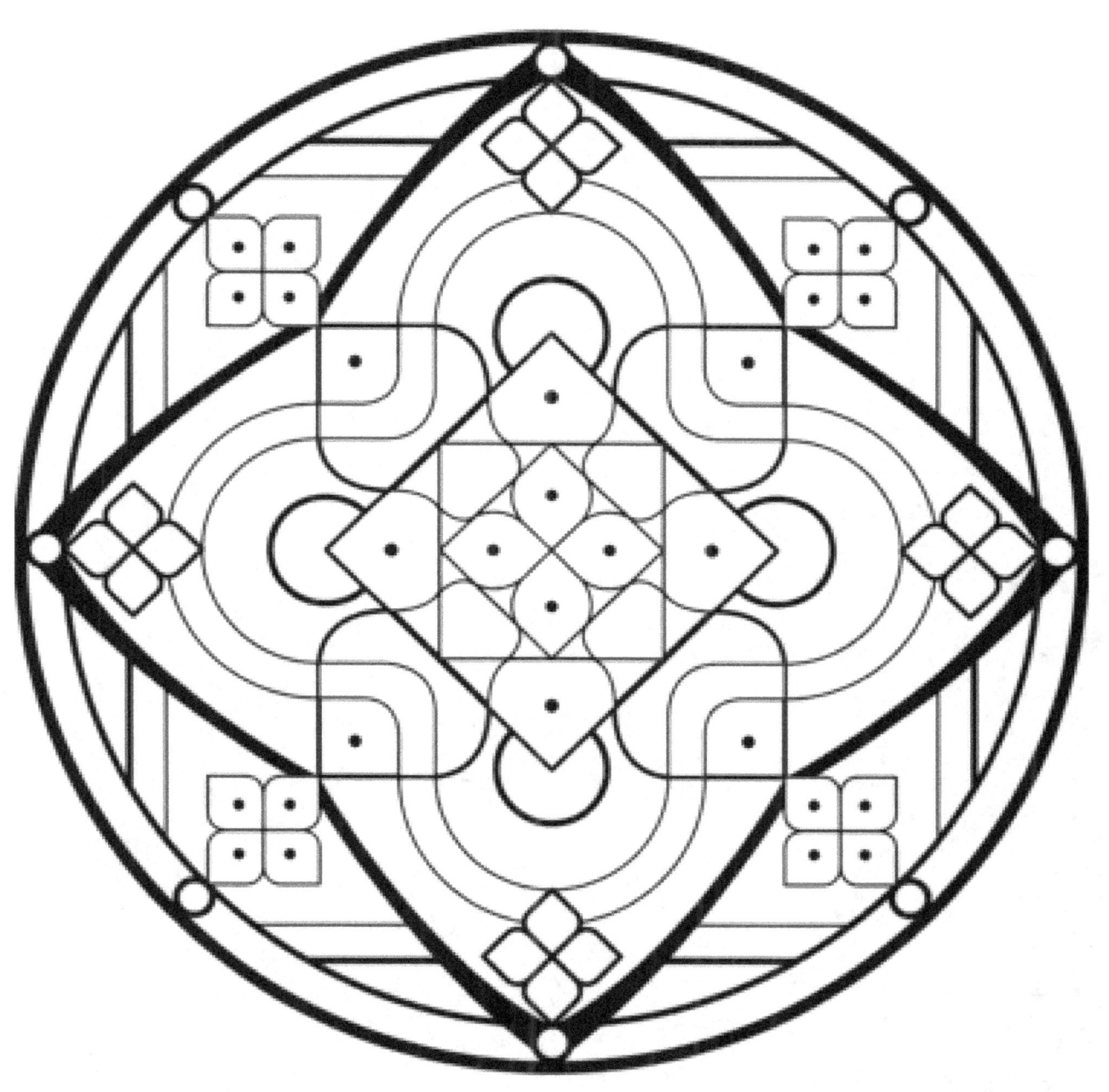

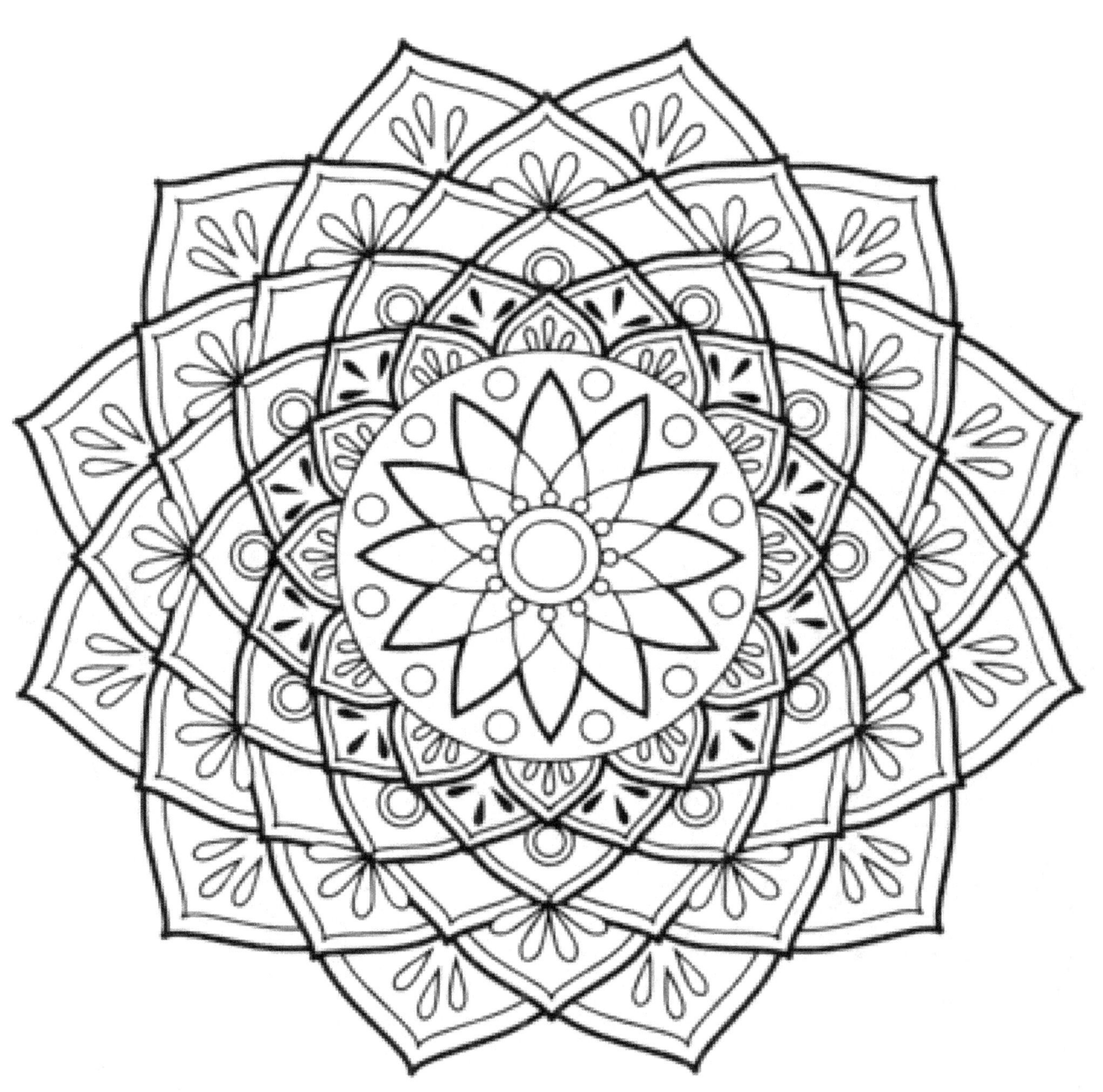

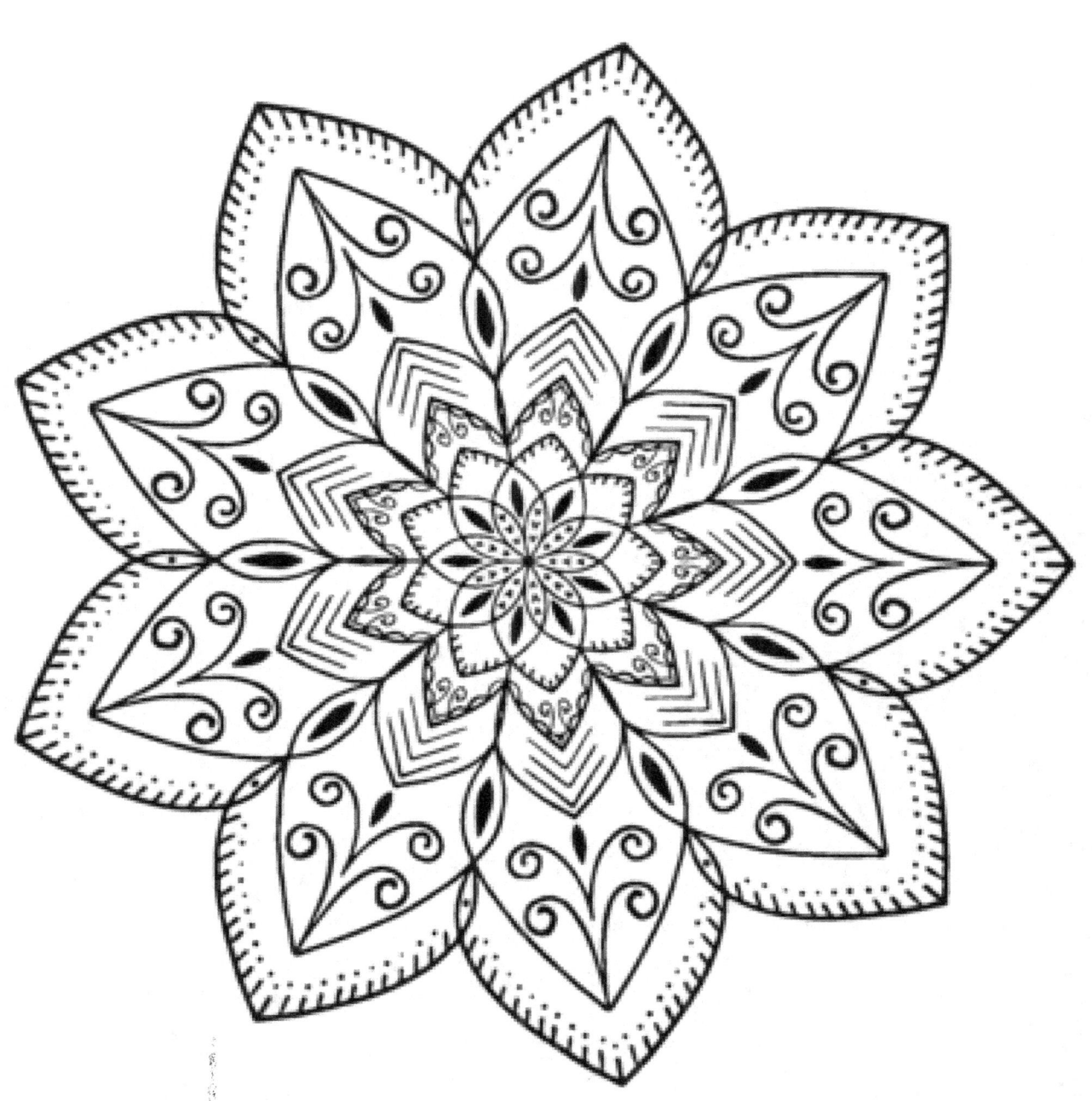

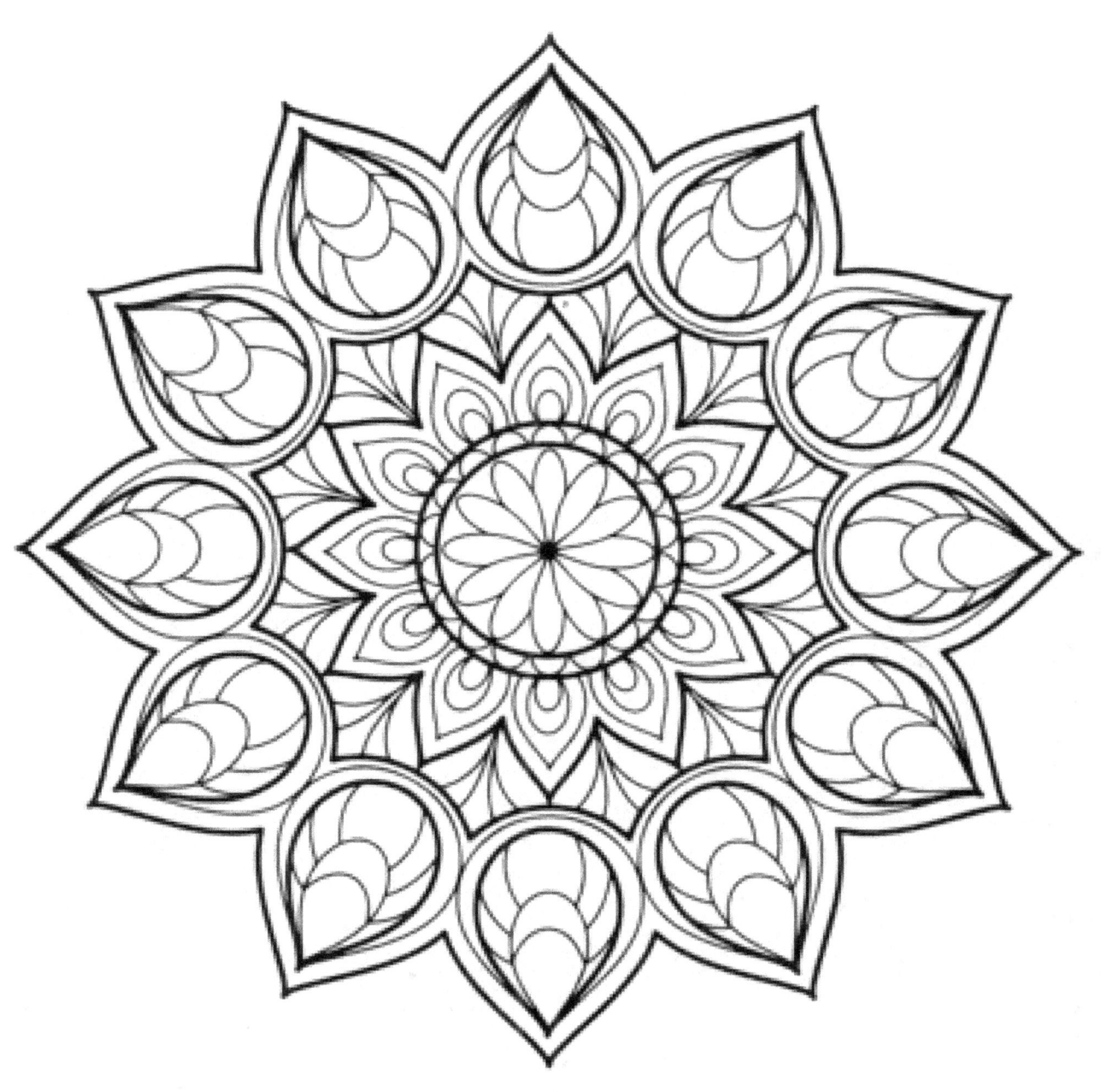

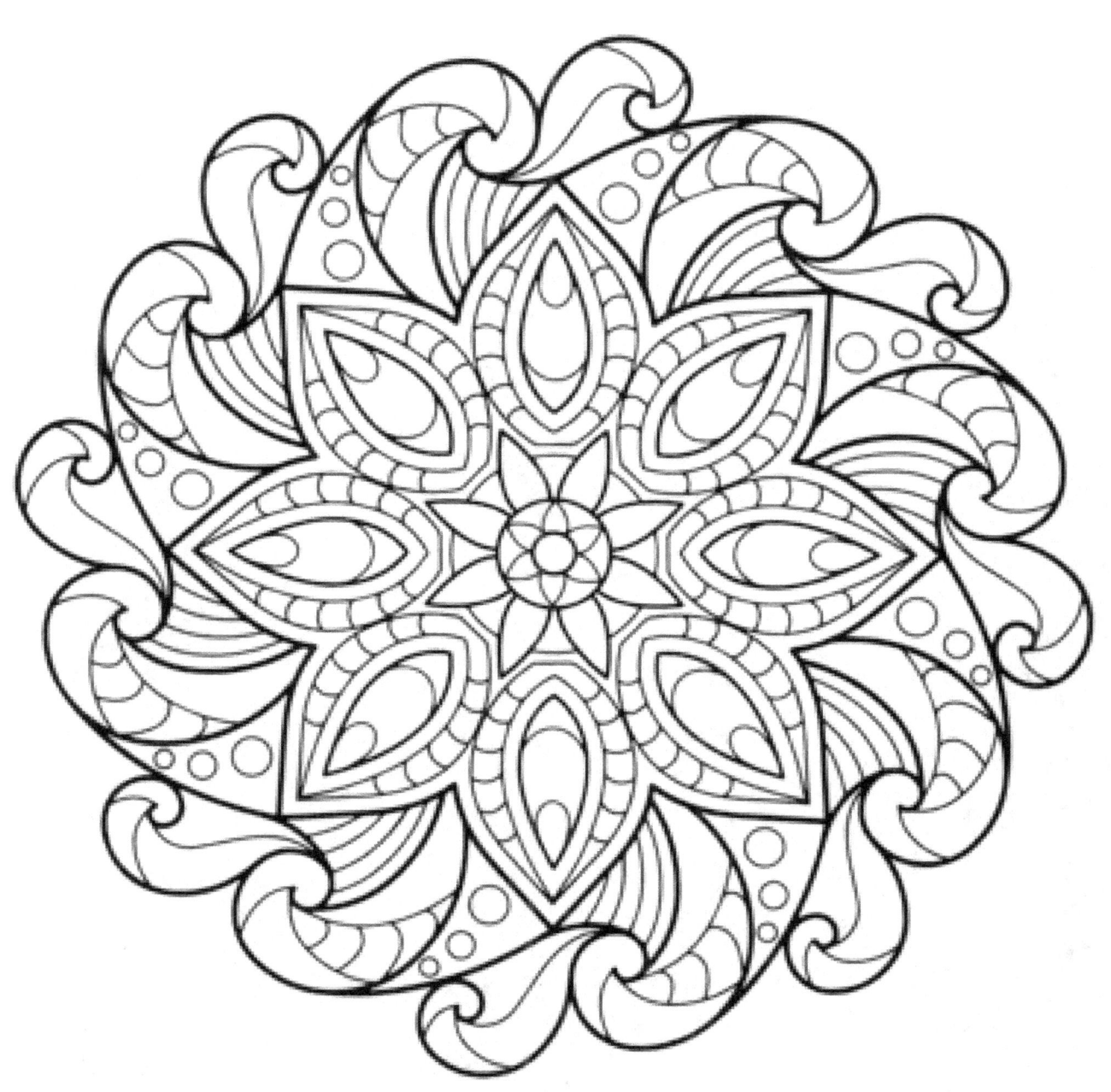

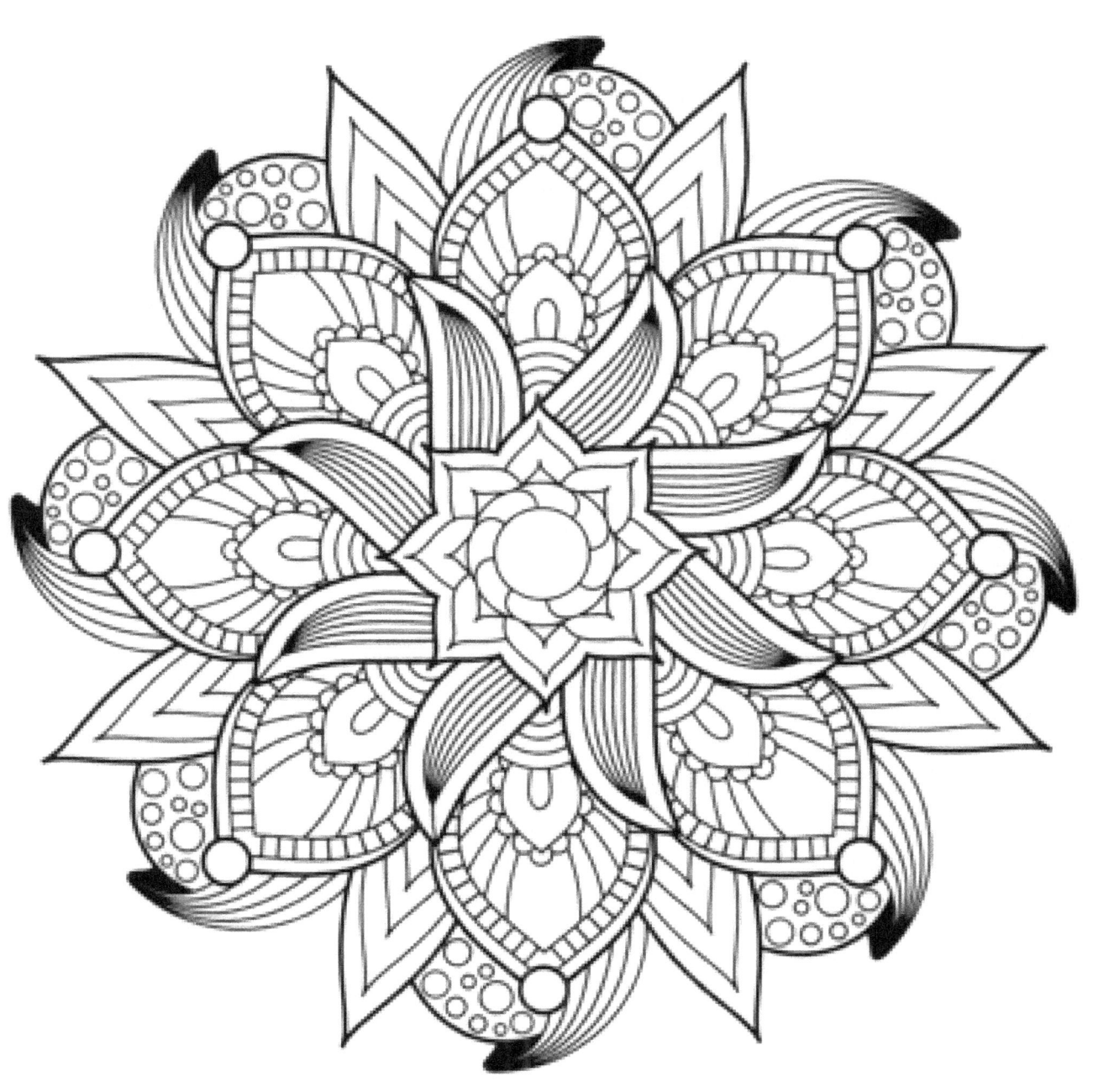

www.ingramcontent.com/pod-product-compliance
Lightning Source LLC
Chambersburg PA
CBHW080609220526
45466CB00010B/3296